WHO'S AFRAID OF VIRGINIA WOOLF?

Necessary Fictions, Terrifying Realities

TWAYNE'S MASTERWORK STUDIES
Robert Lecker, General Editor

WHO'S AFRAID OF VIRGINIA WOOLF?

Necessary Fictions, Terrifying Realities

MATTHEW C. ROUDANÉ

TWAYNE PUBLISHERS • BOSTON
A Division of G. K. Hall & Co.

Who's Afraid of Virginia Woolf?: Necessary Fictions, Terrifying Realities
Matthew C. Roudané

Twayne's Masterwork Studies No. 34

Copyright 1990 by G.K. Hall & Co.
All rights reserved.
Published by Twayne Publishers
A Division of G. K. Hall & Co.
70 Lincoln Street
Boston, Massachusetts 02111

Copyediting supervised by Barbara Sutton
Book production by Patricia D'Agostino
Book design by Barbara Anderson

Typeset in 10/14 Sabon with Albertus display type
by Compositors Corporation

Printed on permanent/durable acid-free paper
and bound in the United States of America

Library of Congress Cataloging-in-Publication Data
Roudané, Matthew Charles, 1953–
    Who's afraid of Virginia Woolf? : necessary fictions, terrifying
realities / Matthew C. Roudané.
        p.   cm. — (Twayne's masterwork studies ; 34)
    Includes bibliographical references.
    ISBN 0-8057-8059-9 (alk. paper). — ISBN 0-8057-8105-6 (pbk. :
alk. paper)
    1. Albee, Edward. 1928–   Who's afraid of Virginia Woolf?
I. Title. II. Series.
PS3551.L25W437   1989
812'54—dc20
                                                        89–36965
                                                            CIP

For Susan and Nickolas

CONTENTS

NOTE ON REFERENCES
AND ACKNOWLEDGMENTS

All references to *Who's Afraid of Virginia Woolf?* are to the Atheneum edition (New York, 1962), with page numbers provided in parentheses. Other works by Edward Albee frequently cited in the text are abbreviated as follows:

AD *The American Dream*
AO *All Over*
BQ *Box and Quotations from Chairman Mao Tse-tung*
CEA *Conversations with Edward Albee* (ed. Philip C. Kolin)
DB *A Delicate Balance*
L *Listening*
TP *The Plays, volume 1*
ZS *The Zoo Story*

Full publication information is provided in the Bibliography.

I am grateful to Edward Albee and Atheneum for permission to quote from selected passages of *Who's Afraid of Virginia Woolf?*, © 1962 by Atheneum.

I wish to thank Edward Albee, who has discussed his work with me over the past several years. I also want to thank Virginia Spencer Carr and Clyde W. Faulkner, Georgia State University, for their professional support of this and other books over the years. Part of this book was supported by a Georgia State University Research Grant, for which I am grateful. Leigh Kirkland Pietschner provided valuable and prompt editorial advice. Special thanks go to my parents, Charles and Orient Roudané; they know their influence on my work. Finally, I wish to thank Susan, my wife, for making all this possible. Once again she took time from her busy career to care for our son when I most needed some time to write and, as always, she provided a welcome reality check.

Edward Albee with the author, 1988.
Photograph by Harrie Burdan.

CHRONOLOGY:

EDWARD ALBEE'S LIFE AND WORKS

1928 Edward Albee born 12 March in Washington, D.C. He is abandoned by his natural parents and is adopted two weeks later by Reed A. and Frances Cotta Albee, who bring him to Larchmont, New York. He is named after his adoptive grandfather, Edward Franklin Albee, part owner of over two hundred vaudeville theaters (the Keith-Albee circuit) across the country.

1939 Attends Rye County Day School, Westchester County, New York, and is expelled—a pattern that will develop as he is sent to a number of different boarding schools.

1940 Attends the Lawrenceville School, Lawrenceville, New Jersey. Writes a three-act sex farce, *Aliqueen*, his first attempt at playwriting.

1943 Dismissed from Lawrenceville. Enrolls in Valley Forge Military Academy, Wayne, Pennsylvania, from which he is also dismissed.

1944 Attends the Choate School, Wallingford, Connecticut, where he begins to write. Encouraged by his English teacher, he continues to write stories, poems, essays, and plays during his years at Choate. During his youth, the Albee home is visited by family friend W. H. Auden; several years later he will meet Thornton Wilder. Both Auden and Wilder read his poetry and, unimpressed, encourage the young Albee to try his hand at something else—perhaps playwriting.

1945 "Eighteen" published in *Kaleidograph*, a Texas literary magazine.

1946 First published play, "Schism," appears in the *Choate Literary Magazine*. Continues to write short poems and attempts a novel. After graduating from Choate, attends Trinity College, Hartford, Connecticut. Acts in Maxwell Anderson's *The Masque of Kings* as Emperor Franz Joseph. After three semesters, is dismissed from college for refusing to attend certain required classes and chapel.

1947	Writes continuity material for music programs on WNYC radio in New York.
1948–1958	Moves to Greenwich Village and works at various jobs: office boy for an advertising agency, salesperson in Bloomingdale's record department, barman in the Manhattan Towers Hotel, Western Union messenger. During this decade he is supported by a trust fund established by his maternal grandmother in 1949. Grandma Cotta will become Grandma in *The American Dream*. During this decade Albee continues to write many plays, none of which have ever been performed or published. Today the manuscripts are held at the New York Public Library and may be seen only after Albee himself grants special permission. They are not intended for performance.
1958	*The Zoo Story.*
1959	First production of *The Zoo Story* at the Schiller Theater Werkstatt, Berlin, 28 September. The play, which had been rejected for performance in the United States, draws rave reviews. Albee attends the Berlin premiere, although he cannot understand German. He receives the Berlin Festival Award.
1960	American production of *The Zoo Story* at the Provincetown Playhouse, New York, 14 January. It is part of a twin bill, the other play being Beckett's *Krapp's Last Tape*. This is a fabulous inspiration to the struggling, unknown young Albee. *The Death of Bessie Smith* is produced at the Schlosspark Theater, Berlin, 21 April. *The Sandbox*, commissioned for the Festival of Two Worlds, Spoleto, Italy, is staged at the Jazz Gallery, New York, 15 April. *Fam and Yam* is produced at the White Barn, Westport, Connecticut, 27 August.
1961	*The American Dream* staged at the York Playhouse, New York, 24 January, and runs for 360 performances. With William Flanagan and James Hinton, Albee co-writes *Bartleby*, an opera based on Melville's short story. *The Sandbox*, starring Sudie Bond as Grandma, is televised. Albee receives the Lola D'Annunzio Award for original playwriting in June. He is awarded a Fulbright professorship to Wurzburg University, Germany.
1962	"Which Theatre Is the Absurd One?" published on 25 February in the *New York Times*. Soon after Albee purchases a second home in Montauk, Long Island, where he still retreats to write in the summers. *Who's Afraid of Virginia Woolf?* produced at the Billy Rose Theatre, New York, 13 October. The play is Albee's first Broadway effort and galvanizes his public reputa-

tion; it goes on to run for 664 performances and eventually receives the Drama Critics' Award, a Tony Award, and numerous other prizes. It is nominated for the Pulitzer Prize but does not win because certain members of the Pulitzer Prize committee find it "a filthy play." Other members who support the play resign in protest. Subsequent press coverage of such controversy, coupled with the play's intensity, only make the play the *cause célèbre* of the theatrical season. The play is censored, even banned in places.

1963   With Richard Barr and Clinton Wilder, establishes the New York Playwrights Unit Workshop to help young writers. Terrence McNally, Lanford Wilson, John Guare, Imamu Amri Baraka, and Sam Shepard, among others, take advantage of this opportunity. *The Ballad of the Sad Café*, an adaptation of Carson McCullers's novella of the same name, is produced at the Martin Beck Theater, New York, 30 October. Near the end of the year Albee travels with John Steinbeck to the Soviet Union and other east European countries as a U.S. Cultural Exchange Visitor.

1964   *Who's Afraid of Virginia Woolf?* debuts in London in February. With Sir John Gielgud and Irene Worth in the leading roles, *Tiny Alice* opens at the Billy Rose Theatre, New York, 29 December. The play causes some controversy because of its baffling quality, although it runs for 167 shows.

1965   *Tiny Alice* wins the New York Drama Critics' Award and a Tony, and Albee receives the Margot Jones Award for helping new dramatists. He also reviews Sam Shepard's *Icarus's Mother* in the *Village Voice*.

1966   Stages *Malcolm*, an adaptation of James Purdy's novel of the same name, which opens at the Shubert Theatre, New York, 11 January, and closes after seven performances. Albee places an ad in the *New York Times* apologizing for the failure and invites audiences to his next play. He buys an old carriage house in Greenwich Village. The Warner Brothers film of *Who's Afraid of Virginia Woolf?*, starring Elizabeth Taylor and Richard Burton as Martha and George, and George Segal and Sandy Dennis as Nick and Honey, is released in July. Although extremely successful the film is banned, censored, and altered in various parts of the country (and the world), often carrying a "for adults only" label. *A Delicate Balance*, which will win the playwright his first Pulitzer Prize, opens 22 September at the Martin Beck Theater, New York. It runs for 132 performances and stars Jessica Tandy and Hume Cronyn. Albee is elected to the National Institute of the Arts at the end of the year. His adaptation (with David Merrick) of Truman Capote's *Breakfast at Tiffany's* opens in December and runs for only four shows.

1967   Awarded Pulitzer Prize for *A Delicate Balance* on 2 May. In June is awarded a D. Litt. from Emerson College, the first of several honorary doctorates he will receive. *Everything in the Garden,* an adaptation of a Giles Cooper play of the same name, opens at the Plymouth Theatre, New York, 29 November, and is performed eighty-four times.

1968   *Box* and *Quotations from Chairman Mao Tse-tung,* two interrelated plays, open on 7 March at the Buffalo Studio Arena Theatre, Buffalo, New York. The plays move on to the Billy Rose Theatre in New York, 30 September, and run for twelve performances.

1971   *All Over* produced at the Martin Beck Theater, New York, 27 March. The play is directed by John Gielgud and stars Jessica Tandy and Colleen Dewhurst for its forty performances.

1972   *All Over* is produced by the Royal Shakespeare Company, London, at the Aldwych Theatre, 31 January.

1973   As part of the "American Film Theatre Series" directs film version of *A Delicate Balance,* which stars Katharine Hepburn, Paul Scofield, Lee Remick, Joseph Cotton, and Kate Reid.

1974   Receives a D. Litt. from one of the schools that expelled him— Trinity College in Hartford.

1975   *Seascape* opens 23 January at the Sam S. Shubert Theatre, New York, and will earn the playwright his second Pulitzer Prize. Albee directs his own work again, which runs for sixty-five shows.

1976   *Who's Afraid of Virginia Woolf?* begins a very successful revival on Broadway in April. By this point Albee directs most of his own work, as he does with this production. The revival stars Colleen Dewhurst and Ben Gazzara. *All Over,* produced by the Hartford Stage Company 28 April, is shown on the public television series, "Theatre in America." Albee receives yet another honorary doctorate from Southhampton College of Long Island, where he delivers the commencement address. *Listening* produced as a radio play for the BBC Radio Three in England and broadcast 28 March. *Counting the Ways* staged at the National Theatre, London, 6 December.

1977   American premiere of *Counting the Ways* and *Listening* at the Hartford Stage Company, Hartford, Connecticut, 28 January.

1978	Directs a troupe staging eight of his one-act plays around the country and in Canada. The production is called "Albee Directs Albee."
1980	*The Lady From Dubuque*, with Irene Worth in the lead, performed at the Morosco Theater, New York, 31 January. The play closes after only twelve shows. In May Albee wins a Gold Medal in Drama from the American Academy and Institute of Arts and Letters; in November he is named one of the directors of the Vivian Beaumont Theater in Lincoln Center.
1981	Stages a controversial and unsuccessful adaptation of *Lolita*, based on Nabokov's novel, 19 March at the Brooks Atkinson Theatre, New York. Starring Donald Sutherland, the play closes after eleven performances. *The Plays*, volume 1, published.
1982	*The Man Who Had Three Arms* staged 4 October at the Goodman Theatre, Chicago.
1983	*The Man Who Had Three Arms* makes its Broadway debut on 5 April at the Lyceum Theatre, only to close after sixteen shows. *The Plays*, volumes 2 and 3, published. On 10 May, *Finding the Sun*, directed by Albee, debuts at the University of Northern Colorado. He is asked to chair the Brandeis University Creative Arts Award Committee and is appointed regents' professor of drama at the University of California, Irvine.
1984	*Walking* premieres 22 May at the University of California, Irvine. Also staged is Albee's *Finding the Sun*.
1985	*Envy*, part of Nagel Jackson's *Faustus in Hell*, produced in January. Albee attends the Budapest Cultural Forum in October where he delivers a speech.
1986	Albee publishes "A World Where Governments Fear the World" in *Dramatists Guild Quarterly* (winter 1986), adapted from the speech he delivered in Budapest in 1985.
1987	Albee is recognized, with Adrienne Rich, for his achievements in the arts at the annual Brandeis University Arts Awards. *Marriage Play* (which Albee directs) debuts at Vienna's English Theatre, Vienna, 10 June.

1

HISTORICAL CONTEXT
The Cultural Landscape

The anger of *Who's Afraid of Virginia Woolf?* reflects Albee's rebellion against a culture whose identity radically transformed during his youth. In the late 1940s and through the 1950s, the young Albee took measure of, and became disenchanted with, the rapidly shifting industrial, social, and historical climate of the United States. A young man in his teens and twenties during this period, Albee felt as perplexed with American culture as would Jerry, his first antihero in *The Zoo Story.*

From 1945 to 1950, unprecedented optimism, buoyed by economic growth, confirmed this country's a priori belief in the beauty of self-reliance, hard work, and democracy. Suddenly we were fulfilling our self-created prophecy as the watchkeepers of the entire free world, a position certified by military and technological triumphs in World War II and sustained by unheard-of economic resurgence. While Albee was being expelled from military school and from one prep school after another, soldiers returned from the war, increasing college enrollments to record-breaking numbers as the G. I. Bill of Rights picked up the tuition tab. Harry Truman sanctioned military assistance to any free nation challenged by communism. George C. Marshall ushered in a plan to reconstruct war-ravaged Europe—Axis and Allied countries alike. The United

Nations was established, meant to underscore our hope for world peace, even as the iron curtain divided Berlin and Mao Tse-tung subjugated China to his tyranny. During these events, the teenage Albee struggled as a novice writer, trying his hand at poetry, the short story, and the novel while growing up in or near New York City. There, he witnessed Broadway's rejuvenation, thanks to Tennessee Williams's *The Glass Menagerie* (1944) and *A Streetcar Named Desire* (1947), and Arthur Miller's *All My Sons* (1947) and *Death of a Salesman* (1949).

A dramatist who would dominate the theater world in the 1960s, Albee's discontent with himself and his culture was fermenting in the 1950s. The 1950s seemed a complacent period, surely a cultural response to the depression in the 1930s and World War II in the 1940s, an anodyne for the two decades of cataclysms that rocked the country. While Albee left the privileged home of his millionaire family for the bohemian life in Greenwich Village during his twenties (largely possible because of a generous trust fund set up by his grandmother), the country spawned the "silent generation" of conformist students, subdivision housing, and the Eisenhower era. Recent biographers of Ike paint a portrait of a far more complex, clever president, but his public image, in memory, remains an emblem for the sleepy, pipe-and-slippers, Ozzie-and-Harriet world Americans elevated to new heights. While Albee felt alone, out of place, a cosmic waif drifting through the 1950s with no discernible purpose, he witnessed the homogenization of America. Television and the first fast-food restaurants, suburbs and barbecues, shopping centers and Little League seemed to dominate the geographical as well as moral landscape. The Interstate Highway System, the most audacious public-works project in our history, further contributed to cultural homogenizing. As real incomes soared to new levels (matched only by the height of the high-finned Cadillacs), Americans celebrated their new wealth and recrudescence through conspicuous consumption. Television, first black and white, then color, enraptured as it anesthetized the country, and television not only joined people of differing regions with an electronic immediacy, but quickly outdistanced radio and the theater as a source of cultural "education" and entertainment. While the youthful Albee grew more introspective, Hula-Hoops and 3-D movies were great fads. Soon after he was expelled from Trinity College in Hartford, Connecticut, Albee would see an American college population preoccupied with stuffing one another into phone booths.

Of course the 1950s were more complex than the banal world implied above. The decade, in fact, appeared as divided and confused as the heroes in *Who's Afraid of Virginia Woolf?*. For Albee would read about the Korean War and our country's ambivalent response to the "conflict." Foreshadowing the social eruptions of the 1960s, the 1950s gave rise to civil-rights protests. Chief Justice Earl Warren altered the judicial system as the Supreme Court sought to alleviate racial injustice in public schools. Albee would read newspapers filled with reports of federal troops in Little Rock, Arkansas, under Eisenhower's orders, trying to enforce desegregation; of Rosa Parks's defiant act of keeping her seat on the bus; of Martin Luther King, Jr.'s subsequent boycott of Montgomery, Alabama's bus system. There was also some bothersome little skirmish brewing in Vietnam in the 1950s. The Soviets invaded Hungary and Nixon held court with Khrushchev in the "kitchen debate." Albee's growing lover's quarrel with the world only increased as he lived through McCarthyism and saw Clifford Odets, Elia Kazan, Lillian Hellman, and countless other writers or "subversives" brought before the House Un-American Activities Committee. Fear of Alger Hiss, the Rosenbergs, and Communist spies assumed hysterical proportions. And while many great contemporary American writers were establishing themselves in the 1950s—J. D. Salinger and Saul Bellow, Adrienne Rich and Lorraine Hansberry—the conservative social ambiance put a damper even on those writers valorized by their past glories: while Elvis Presley, hips gyrating, entranced the nation with rock and roll in 1956, Arthur Miller endured hostile questioning during the McCarthy "witch hunt" trials; while the consumer society elevated material acquisition to an exalted position, Allen Ginsberg howled, James Baldwin exiled himself, and Jack Kerouac hit the road—all while the writer within Albee yearned to create art. During the 1950s, Albee said, he felt "desperate" because he might not "make it" in any profession. Before the decade was out, he would compose *The Zoo Story* as a thirtieth birthday present to himself.[1]

On 4 October 1957—Albee was twenty-nine—the Soviet Union

stunned America. With the successful launching of *Sputnik,* the Russians conquered space, an achievement hailed as the most significant technological feat since the Americans developed the atomic bomb. *Sputnik* mystified the American psyche. The sphere-shaped object flew faster, higher, and was (ten times) larger than any American-made spacecraft: 18,000 m.p.h., 560-mile altitude capability, mysterious in its tightly guarded contents—these were incredible facts. While U.S. scientists labored with tiny, yet-to-be-launched space probes, the Russians basked in what was perceived by the world as mastery of earthly and outer-space affairs. Suddenly America's unquestioned position as the world's superpower was undermined technologically and psychologically.

The moment affected writers as well. No other event "so deeply influenced contemporary thinking as the launching of the first Sputnik," points out Mas'ud Zavarzadeh in *The Mythopoeic Reality.* Even the very methods of fiction-making were radicalized "since about 1957—the year the Soviet Union's Sputnik shook America and almost overnight changed the cold war of ideological opposition between the two postwar superpowers into a planetary polarization between Man and Machine."[2] Zavarzadeh theorizes about the postwar American "nonfiction" novel, but the point is that, for Albee, the certainties, the reliabilities of past notions of objective reality were no longer safe guides. Such radical transformations, of course, manifested themselves in the earlier twentieth century too. As "a predictable world, tied securely to a familiar past, began to give way to a sense of larger uncertainty, of radical change," writes Alice van Buren Kelley of Virginia Woolf's post–World War I world, "it forced people to confront the fragility of life and opened the way for the expectation of the new, the unpredictable."[3] Precisely the same psychological as well as aesthetic shifts that had altered Virginia Woolf's post-Victorian world would alter the cultural milieu in which Albee would compose his masterwork, but, in context of the nuclear age, *Sputnik,* and other historical changes, he would do so with even a greater sense of the utter precariousness of human existence. As Albee said in 1963, "the existentialist and post-existentialist revaluation of the nature of reality . . . gained the importance that it has now as a result of the bomb at Hiroshima" (*CEA,* 36).

Indeed, in the months before Albee took Broadway by storm with *Who's Afraid of Virginia Woolf?*, U.S.–Soviet relations headlined the news. For six terrifying days in October 1962, as the cast went through final rehearsals for the play, Khrushchev and Kennedy brought us to the brink of nuclear war. The Soviets had shipped missiles to Cuba, America threatened military intervention, and Khrushchev blinked—the crisis was diffused when the missiles were ordered back to the Soviet Union. After Korea, *Sputnik,* and Khrushchev's victory in the Vienna summit meeting with Kennedy, the Cuban missile crisis was resolved in a triumphant moment for America. And yet, as new-frontier optimism swept the land and *Who's Afraid of Virginia Woolf?* captured Broadway, Kennedy also authorized sending American troops and military advisors to Vietnam. America was becoming more aware of its faults, but still seemed energized by a naive ebullience and unwavering faith in the myth of the American dream. The pot of gold at the end of the rainbow surely loomed just beyond the horizon, most Americans felt, even as Albee lamented in 1960 that the people of the United States had substituted "artificial for real values in our society," and that his theater was "a stand against the fiction that everything in this slipping land of ours is peachy-keen" (*AD,* 53–54). These were brazen words, given the conservative climate of the time, words only lunatics, lovers, and poets (might) get away with articulating. Until 22 November 1963 at noontime—when an assassin's bullets shattered Camelot—America reveled in its idealism, although with *The Zoo Story, The American Dream, The Death of Bessie Smith,* and *Who's Afraid of Virginia Woolf?* Albee had lodged a dissenting voice of tremendous theatrical power.

THE THEATRICAL LANDSCAPE

The theatrical landscape of America was as divided as the culture dramatized by its playwrights. A volatile mix of theatrical forces—economic, social, political, aesthetic, historical—conspired to make Albee's Broadway debut especially timely. "To many people," observes C. W. E. Bigsby, "the American theatre seemed threatened with imminent collapse, while the great dramatists who had sustained the international reputation of American drama for so long were no longer in evidence."[4] In other words, Broadway had reached a low point by the time *Who's Afraid of Virginia Woolf?* made its epochal premiere that Saturday evening, 13 October 1962. As Bigsby implies, Broadway audiences were seeking some sort of original American play that could rekindle the excitement and metaphysical seriousness generated by Eugene O'Neill's *Long Day's Journey into Night,* Arthur Miller's *Death of a Salesman,* and Tennessee Williams's *A Streetcar Named Desire,* and would match the technical precision of the exemplary British dramatists. Albee suddenly found himself "as the man singled out to take on the burden formerly carried on by O'Neill, Miller, and Williams,"[5] a position which surely thrilled the young playwright but with which he never felt fully comfortable. Essentially an Off Broadway dramatist, Albee experienced the pressures of one anointed to redeem the American Broadway theater. And so Albee's masterwork somehow saved Broadway from collapsing: *Who's Afraid of Virginia Woolf?* ran before packed houses for 664 performances; turned into one of the most lucrative films of 1966 for Warner Brothers; and went on to dominate the theater world in the 1960s with successful revivals. This play did nothing less than reinvent the American theater.

THE ETHOS OF BROADWAY

Despite the rather pathetic state of Broadway, there were some extremely popular plays staged during the 1962–63 Broadway season. Sumner Arthur Long's comedy *Never Too Late,* Richard Sheridan's eighteenth-century comedy *The School for Scandal,* and *Oliver!,* a musical adaptation of Charles Dickens's *Oliver Twist,* attracted sizable and largely supportive audiences. The Actors' Studio Theatre staged two well-received revivals—O'Neill's *Strange Interlude* and George Bernard Shaw's *Too Good to Be True.* Moreover, several commanding holdovers from other seasons still drew enormous crowds during the 1962–63 season. *The Sound of Music* was still attracting audiences after 1,424 performances while *Mary, Mary* weighed in next with 977 showings. Other successful shows included *How to Succeed in Business without Really Trying* (679 performances); *A Man for All Seasons* (638); *No Strings* (506); and *A Funny Thing Happened on the Way to the Forum* (447). Several other major productions that finally closed during the season of *Who's Afraid of Virginia Woolf?* were *My Fair Lady*—after six years and 2,715 shows; *Camelot*—after 873 performances; and *Carnival*—after 719 shows. Clearly, on one level Broadway exhibited a degree of vitality.

But as much of this sampling of the early 1960s Broadway fare suggests, mainstream American theater in New York City seemed woefully inadequate in qualitative terms. While theaters across Europe were typically staging plays imbued with ethical import and political textures, many Broadway theaters tended to produce superficial works. The "messianic" revolts that Robert Brustein, in *The Theatre of Revolt*, located in such great contemporary European dramatists as Adamov, Ionesco, Anouilh, Genet, Brecht, and others, were not to be found in the commercially based Broadway aesthetic. If a play were "safe"—if it would not offend too many and would sell at the gate—it might see a healthy stage life. Experiments in performance theory and practice, politically extreme works, plays that deliberately challenged the conservative tastes of Broadway were found beyond the Great White Way—in university theaters, regional theaters, and Off Broadway. From a purely business standpoint, such Off Broadway productions did not (nor did they ever aspire to) earn profits. Thus, paradoxically enough, while Broadway audiences were anxiously searching for the Great New Playwright, they also preferred *Mary, Mary* to *Waiting for Godot*. A Broadway play's vitality often seemed measured in commercial value, a play's worth directly corresponding to its ratings at the gate. True, there were occasional revivals of masterpieces of world drama, but predictable works—plays appealing to those paying for entertainment—diluted Broadway. Two prominent American dramatists, one from the older generation, the second a newer voice, partially explain the limitations of Broadway. "If you hand a producer a piece that offends a significant portion of the Broadway audience, not to speak of the critics," Arthur Miller observes, "he'll think two or three times before putting it on. You are in that way bound to one level of consciousness. It's not a new thing; my argument with our theater on that level is that it's constricted to a degree greater than I have ever known in my lifetime. It is very important that people not have to pay $40 to get into the theater, because if they pay $40, they're probably not going to want what I am writing . . . . A forty dollar ticket brooks no philosophies, tends toward triviality."[6] And David Mamet, a more recent voice in American drama (and film), agrees with Miller: the playwright on Broadway often appeals "to people who aint never going to come back, who don't really have any expectations but know they better get something for their $45. So we show them a hundred people tap dancing on stage instead of *Death of a Salesman*."[7]

So when Albee packed up his talents from Off Broadway and journeyed (as Jerry in *The Zoo Story* might put it) a very long distance out of his way to Broadway in 1962, plays "bound to one level of consciousness" were saturating the market. And yet even the dominant "safe" plays were beset by financial disaster. Over $6 million (in 1962–63 dollars) were lost to Broadway flops. Nor were such failures confined to new works, avant-garde experiments, or even sentimental musicals. Tennessee Williams's *The Milk Train Doesn't Stop Here Anymore* (sixty-nine performances in the 1962–63 season); Sidney Kingsley's *Night Life* (sixty-three shows); Bertolt Brecht's *Mother Courage and Her Children* (fifty-two); William Inge's *Natural Affection* (thirty-six); and Lillian Hellman's *My Mother, My Father, and Me* (only seventeen performances) all "failed" at one of Broadway's chief gauges of "success": the box office. Thus it is hardly astonishing to find Daniel Blum, in his *Theatre World: Season 1962–1963*, concluding: "The 1962–63 season was a disastrous one both financially and artistically."[8]

The uneasy state of Broadway that Albee would have to confront was in many ways not new. Indeed, its decline in the early 1960s was part of a larger, dismal pattern of decadence harkening back to the earlier twentieth century. Broadway enjoyed its best days from the 1899–1900 season, when there were eighty-seven new productions, through the 1927–28 season, which spawned an all-time high of 264 new shows. However, from the 1930s onward, the number of new productions in New York City persistently diminished. Three decades before *Who's Afraid of Virginia Woolf?*, there were 174 new productions in New York

City; two decades before, eighty; and one decade previous, fifty-four. Two seasons before Albee entered Broadway, only forty-eight new productions were staged, an all-time low to that point, and by 1962–63, the number crept only to fifty-four new productions.[9]

CULTURAL ATTITUDES TOWARD THE THEATER

Americans have cultivated, historically and emotionally, an intensely ambivalent attitude toward the theater. During the Puritan era plays were often perceived as immoral spectacles, and some actors and actresses faced jail sentences for their "sacrilegious" performances. Shakespeare's scripts were radically edited to conform to Puritan doctrinal ethics. In the nineteenth century, vaudeville productions grew to assume a popular role but, critically and aesthetically, America produced no dramatists who could even come close to the quality of writers and poets such as Emerson, Dickinson, Poe, Melville, Whitman, or Twain. Further, the antics of audiences within theater houses often exceeded the action of the plays themselves. Frances Trollope, in her *Domestic Manners of the Americans* (1827), recalled her frequent visits to theaters in Cincinnati, Philadelphia, and other United States cities, and, as Walter J. Meserve reports in *Heralds of Promise,* she "was never pleased." Meserve says of Trollope's reactions to American audiences: "The climax of her disenchantment came at the Chatham Theatre in New York where in the first row of the dress box she observed a 'lady performing the most maternal office possible.' Mrs. Trollope's observations and reactions, however, clearly identified the theatre at this time, and throughout the period editors of literary magazines would occasionally question why anybody would want to write for this theatre." Meserve therefore correctly surmises, "the playwright's task was not easy. Just as the times and attitudes provided material for American dramatists, the public mood also created great barriers to their progress. Not simply antagonistic toward theatre in general, people placed those barricades specifically and deliberately in the pathway of a developing American drama, ironically prohibiting the emergence of a dramatic literature during this recognized period

[1829-1849] of national emphasis." Meserve pinpoints the alliance of public and private cultural attitudes that discouraged American playwrights from refining their native stage. "For numerous reasons relating to the temperament of the people and their prevailing moods—elitism, anti-intellectualism, religious prejudice, a devotion to work coupled with a lack of time for leisure, a disparate population without traditions of theatre attendance—American dramatists were not encouraged."[10]

Such studies as Arthur Hopson Quinn's *A History of American Drama from the Beginning to the Civil War,* Meserve's *An Emerging Entertainment: The Drama of the American People to 1828* and *Heralds of Promise,* and Brenda Murphy's *American Realism and American Drama, 1880-1940* outline a growing American theater whose identity was evolving long before the twentieth century. In the eighteenth century, Judith Sargent Murray, often writing under the pseudonym "Constantia," may have been the first American composer of plays and the first American woman playwright to see her work staged professionally. Her feminist visions are apparent in *The Gleaner,* a collection of plays published in 1798. Such nineteenth-century playwrights as John Howard Payne, Samuel Woodworth, and Mordecai M. Noah, as well as their subsequent torchbearers who composed during the early years of the twentieth century, James A. Hern, Susan Glaspell, and Clyde Fitch, were all dedicated to forging an American dramatic heritage, although their creative efforts sometimes were closer to craft than art.

The very essence of *live* theater adds to its sometimes ephemeral nature, and perhaps explains the American audience's historical and emotional ambivalence toward its plays and playwrights. If a play draws negative reviews and loses its initial audience, it may be consigned to oblivion. Historically, American audiences often base their thumbs-up-thumbs-down mentality of the theater on the reviewers' judgments as much as on their own perceptions, or on the merits of the play itself. As Frank Rich suggested in 1984, there still remains "the widespread perception that . . . American theater no longer plays a central part of our cultural ferment," even though we have numerous "playwrights who write about issues that matter—or who connect with the rest of our literature, past and present—or who swim with the modernist and postmodernist currents of international art."[11] More recently, Martin Esslin addressed the problem concerning "the marginality of serious drama and theatre in the national consciousness and culture."[12] The Broadway that received Albee mirrored just such an ambivalent cultural attitude. No wonder Albee, writing in the *New York Times*, called Broadway the true theater of the absurd.

It is difficult to delineate precisely the beginnings of an American drama, but many scholars turn to the one person who undoubtedly commanded world attention for, and brought dignity to, the American stage, Eugene O'Neill. Americans had to wait until O'Neill, writing plays for the Provincetown Players in 1916, created a truly original native voice, one that would establish modern American drama as a qualitative genre. Despite O'Neill's stature, and the contributions of Glaspell, Fitch, and later Lillian Hellman, Langston Hughes, Clare Boothe, James Baldwin, Tennessee Williams, Arthur Miller, and Albee, American theater continued to struggle for its identity and sense of aesthetic and ethical purpose. More recent voices in American drama—Sam Shepard, David Mamet, Marsha Norman, Maria Irene Fornes, Richard Foreman, Lanford Wilson, Imamu Amiri Baraka, Charles Fuller, Ntosake Shange, Megan Terry, Tina Howe—continue to struggle with, and enhance, the stage in a culture that still seems at odds with its own theater. In many respects, Albee provided the necessary artistic fix American theater sought in the 1960s, an infusion that would elevate the American theatrical imagination and help a newer generation of playwrights.

2

THE IMPORTANCE OF THE WORK

Ever since Antigone challenged Creon in Sophocles' *Antigone*, Oedipus discovered the appalling source of the plague paralyzing Thebes in *Oedipus Tyrannus*, and Lysistrata orchestrated the sexual strike in Aristophanes' *Lysistrata*, audiences have been enlightened (or at least have had the opportunity to be ennobled) by the militantly civilizing influence of dramatic confrontation and commitment. Euripides of course knew too well about the civic function of the theater—*The Bacchae* and *The Trojan Women* historicized the spiritual slippage of the body politic. Despite the relative newness of *Who's Afraid of Virginia Woolf?* there is an ancient quality about the asymmetries and psychic dislocations embodied within Albee's masterwork. More recently, Arthur Miller highlights the civilizing influence of ancient Greek and Elizabethan drama, a quality that Miller says shapes contemporary theater: "See how the plays that we call great have made us somehow more civilized. The great Greek plays taught the western mind law. They taught the western mind how to settle tribal conflicts without murdering each other. The great Shakespearean plays set up structures of order which became part of our mental equipment. In the immense love stories, the wonderful comedies, there's all sorts of color. But back of these great plays is a civic function. The author was really a poet-philospher."[1] Through its presentation of destruction and tentative redemption, *Who's Afraid of Virginia Woolf?* embodies precisely the kind of civilizing dimension to which Miller alludes; through its presentation of immense disorder, the play reflects its own "structures of order" that have since been infused within our contemporary "mental equipment"; and through the confluence of public and private experiences, the play attains the universal validity that Aristotle finds essential for all great art. Behind the contemporaneity of the play, then, lie some of the primal furies shaping Sophoclean tragedy, Aristophanic comedy, and Elizabethan histories. And the overall influence, forged from the chrysalis of the performing arts, is militantly civilizing.

Surely part of the play's greatness emanates from its sheer theatricality: few if any American dramatists had ever spectacularized a work that embodied such a constellation of heightened emotion and force. But the play's greatness lies in something far beyond its surface explosiveness. The play's renown has to do with its multiple layers of dramatic voices and philosophic textures, a quality that rises above an American theatrical landscape to capture universal human experiences. Time, place, setting, characters—the play stages the particulars of men and women interacting within, in the Aristotelian sense, twenty-fours. But the play also has a timelessness to it. While exploring the details of these people in this place at this time, the play quickly transcends local history and geographical place; at the same time, the play explores those very historical factors and national locales that are wedded to twentieth-century American culture. The private experience of George and Martha define, for Albee, the public issues of a nation and, finally, of human existence itself. The words retain a permanent significance, especially when the play is viewed against the backdrop of what Herbert Blau calls "the alluring or exemplary images of a collective past."[2] *Who's Afraid of Virginia Woolf?* may be held as a classic text because the pastness of its past always reinvents itself in the present, and as such addresses contemporary issues—much the way ancient Greek drama centered on timeless issues and ideas.

Who's Afraid of Virginia Woolf? has a multivalent quality. The play speaks to us on several levels simultaneously, fulfilling Shelley's famous poetic injunction that art pleases, delights, and instructs. Like all great masterworks of drama and literature, this play quickly assumes a larger-than-life texture, its hyperkinetic interactions and mysteriousness underscoring its emotional immediacy, its spiritual intensity. The mimetic energy of George and Martha presents something valid and truthful about contemporary American culture and American thought, and the ways in which the individual sometimes conducts him or herself privately. *Who's Afraid of Virginia Woolf?*, whether in performance, text, or film, reflects the sweep and play of a nation thinking (or not thinking) in front of itself, or a culture seeking to locate its identity through the ritualized action and incantatory language implicit in live theater. "The theatre is the most public of arts," writes C. W. E. Bigsby. "It offers the opportunity of acting out anxieties and fears which are born in conflict between private needs and public values."[3] Albee's masterwork acts out precisely such "anxieties" and "fears."

After seeing or reading *Who's Afraid of Virginia Woolf?*, an audience may in all fairness question certain scenes or particular exchanges, but the overall presentation seems thoroughly convincing. If the play has not endured fully John Dryden's "test of time," it nonetheless sparkles because, for many, it has become what George calls "a survival kit," a culturally coded experience that stages certain a priori attitudes germane to human relationships. On a private level, the play defines the anxieties of two couples and, by extension, all those involved in intimate relationships. On a public level, the play becomes what Kenneth Burke calls "equipment for living."

In its ontological purity, *Who's Afraid of Virginia Woolf?* reflects Albee's awareness of the past modern dramatic heritage. Sexual tensions, combative alliances, divided loyalties, linguistic richness, acerbic repartee, dramaturgic experiment—these elements coalesce in the play, just as they had in Strindberg's *The Dance of Death,* Shaw's *Heartbreak House,* Ibsen's *Hedda Gabler,* Beckett's *Waiting for Godot,* and Pinter's *The Lover.* While demonstrating the author's sensitivity to the pastness of the past, *Who's Afraid of Virginia Woolf?* also highlights Albee's individual talent to rework, indeed, reinvent the dramatic conventions in a wholly original work of art.

The Importance of the Work

The writers he most admires, John Barth has said, are those who "are not only alive to the ideas in the air, but responsible for those ideas being in the air."[4] In *Who's Afraid of Virginia Woolf?*, Albee earns the kind of admiration which Barth finds so important: the play embodies universal psychological experiences while contributing to our deeper awareness of primal familial relationships. The play objectifies unconscious emotions as well as civic duties. Barth also identifies what inevitably lies at the heart of the creative process, "passionate virtuosity": the writer's ideal fusion, in the Coleridgean sense, of idea and image, intellect and emotion.[5] Albee's technical precision and emotional honesty elevate *Who's Afraid of Virginia Woolf?*, and through the mysterious transcendence implicit in serious art, achieve greatness.

3

CRITICAL RECEPTION

Controversy and Albee go hand in hand. Indeed, the only detectable consistency in Albee scholarship is its lack of consistency. Any study of three decades of books, articles, and reviews reveals the balkanization of Albee criticism, the detractor's fevered attack leavened by the supporter's heated defense. From *The Zoo Story* onward, Albee's plays provoke sharply divided critical opinions whose only shared feature is that they seem as mightily opposed as the characters in *Who's Afraid of Virginia Woolf?*. His masterwork only exacerbated the critical battles. The play earned Albee the reputation of being a nihilist, social protester, moralist, allegorist, parodist, dramatic innovator, affirmative existentialist, charlatan, or absurdist. Whether perceived as an historicized account of the decline of Western civilization or as "an elaborate metaphor for what Albee sees as the willing substitution of fantasy for reality, the destructive and dangerous infantilising of the imagination and the moral being by fear,"[1] *Who's Afraid of Virginia Woolf?* has invited, deflected, and absorbed an incredible number of interpretations.

Reviewers questioned Albee's status as a major dramatist, despite the notoriety of *The Zoo Story* and *The American Dream*. *The Sandbox, Fam and Yam,* and *The Death of Bessie Smith* (all produced in 1960) are important works insofar as they reveal Albee's emerging unity of vision and skill as an acerbic dialogist, but they are hardly major plays. They bear the growing pains of a new playwright sorting through autobiographical, ideological, and technical concerns. Albee, very much a product of Off Broadway, was viewed as a promising but untested composer. Was he yet another American playwright with but one or two good plays in his repertoire? Were those who praised him, perhaps in their eagerness to anoint the Next American Playwright, too hasty in their accolades? Would Albee, like his Off Broadway contemporaries Jack Gelber, Jack Richardson, and Kenneth H. Brown, fade after a promising start? Albee had not fulfilled two requirements, the Broadway reviewers felt, to ascend to "major" dramatist ranking: he had yet to compose a full-length play and had yet to stage a play on Broadway.

Albee knew such requirements were superficial, based largely on money and mass popularity rather than substance. He emphatically argued the point the Sunday before *Who's Afraid of Virginia Woolf?* opened at the Billy Rose:

> Everybody knows that Off Broadway, in one season, puts on more fine plays than Broadway does in any five seasons. Everybody knows that Beckett, Genet and Brecht . . . are more important playwrights than almost anybody writing on Broadway today. . . . I do know that, uptown [Broadway], 'success' is so often equated with cash while, downtown [Off Broadway], value does not always have a dollar sign attached. . . . Nonetheless, I am told by some of the cognoscenti that if this play [*Who's Afraid of Virginia Woolf?*] is a success it will be a more important success than the others, and that if it is a failure the failure will be more disastrous than it could be downtown. It may be so, but I can't quite get it through my head why.[2]

Who's Afraid of Virginia Woolf? would ultimately change reservations voiced by reviewers and would unquestionably ratify Albee's place in the American literary canon. In a series of events that surely exceeded the playwright's expectations, the play went on to enjoy a wildly successful stage life here and abroad. Finally, it seemed, a qualitative voice emerged to help Tennessee Williams and Arthur Miller, whose contributions in the 1960s were less than satisfying, sustain the modern American dramatic heritage established by Eugene O'Neill. Albee suddenly found himself valorized. Today his first full-length Broadway effort ranks with some of the classics of American theater—Wilder's *The Skin of Our Teeth*, O'Neill's *Long Day's Journey into Night*, Williams's *A Streetcar Named Desire*, and Miller's *Death of a Salesman*.

Realism and theatricalism, a fusion of the illusion of reality and dramaturgic invention, crystallize in *Who's Afraid of Virginia Woolf?*. Its relentless verbal dueling, Strindbergian sexual tension, and unexpected exorcism within a claustrophobic set generate tremendous excitement and outrage. "The quarrel over *The American Dream* had scarcely died down when Albee exploded a veritable bomb," writes Gilbert Debusscher in *Edward Albee: Tradition and Renewal*, the first of many books on the playwright to appear. "*Who's Afraid of Virginia Woolf?* immediately became the subject of the most impassioned controversies, the object of criticism and accusation which recall the storms over the first plays of Ibsen and, closer to our own time, Beckett and Pinter. If we are able to examine this play today with more serenity, we are nonetheless forced to acknowledge its content might well have outraged the orthodox public of Broadway."[3]

THE REVIEWS

Those coming to the play for the first time found it exciting to read the initial reviews. If nothing else, Albee's masterpiece inspired theatergoers to react. "Only a fortnight after its opening at the Billy Rose Theater it has piled up an astonishing impact," reports one reviewer in the *New York Times*. "You can tell from the steady stream of letters it has precipitated. Elated, argumentative and vitriolic, they have been pouring across my desk and, no doubt, into the offices of my colleagues. Whether they admire or detest the play, theatergoers cannot see it and shrug it off. They burn with an urge to approve or differ. They hail the play's electricity and condemn it as obscene. . . . The public is aroused."[4]

Critical Reception

Many reviewers attacked the play for its heightened volatility and allegedly destructive nature. In one of the more hysterical accounts, Robert Coleman writes, "[It is] a sick play about sick people. They are neurotic, cruel and nasty. They really belong in a sanitarium for the mentally ill rather than on a stage. This sordid and cynical dip into depravity is in three lengthy and repetitious acts. . . . We do not enjoy watching the wings being torn from human flies."[5] Robert Brustein finds it "an ambitious play" but feels it "collapses" because of the son-myth.[6] Harold Clurman, acknowledging Albee's "superbly virile and pliant" dialogue, nonetheless concludes that "the pessimism and rage" of the play are "immature"[7]; Diana Trilling contends that "the 'message' of Mr. Albee's play couldn't be more terrible: life is nothing, and we must have the courage to face our emptiness without fear."[8] For Richard Schechner, the play celebrates decadent values, embracing "self-pity, drooling, womb-seeking weakness" and emerges as an "escape into morbid fantasy."[9] Many felt that, as one reviewer put it, the entire play is "just not believable."[10] Richard A. Duprey calls it "one of the most bitter plays ever penned" and thinks that the play "is a monstrous and clever charade—a foul and puerile nightmare,"[11] while John McCarten simply dismisses the work as "vulgar mishmash."[12]

There were, of course, an astonishing number of favorable reviews. J. C. Trewin admits the play is "cruel," but finds it filled with "savage comedy,"[13] and Richard Watts claims it is "the most shattering drama I have ever seen since O'Neill's 'Long Day's Journey into Night.' "[14] John Gassner, a member of the Pulitzer Prize jury who would later resign in protest of the play's being denied the award, says the play is "*the* negative play to end all negative plays, yet also a curiously compassionate . . . and exhilarating one."[15] In *Newsweek,* Mel Gussow argues that the play "is a splendidly acted, electrically staged (by Alan Schneider), brilliantly original work of art—an excoriating theatrical experience, surging with shocks of recognition and dramatic fire. It will be igniting Broadway for some time to come."[16]

Such radically differing reviews capture the vitriolic early responses to the play. The controversy reached a high point when certain members of the Pulitzer Prize committee refused to bestow the award the play had so clearly earned because, in the words of one committee member, it was "a filthy play."[17] In turn, other members who supported Albee's nomination resigned from the committee in protest. Controversy begot more controversy. "In 1963 the Pulitzer Prize jurors voted *Who's Afraid of Virginia Woolf?* the prize and then the trustees, all 15 of them, got together," Albee mused in 1967. "They were wheeled and carted in, and they had decided by an eight to seven vote that *Who's Afraid of Virginia Woolf?* was too controversial, or too dirty, or something. And so they overrode the jurors. And then it turned out—which I found the only interesting thing—that of the eight who voted against it, four had neither read nor seen it. So I don't know whether this is my first Pulitzer Prize or my second" (*CEA*, 92). In any event, the furor over Albee's being denied the award only enhanced, in the public's eye, his reputation for controversy and somehow made him, like so many young artists in the 1960s, seem like one of those Angry Young Men who would always be tangling with the conservative (as it was called then) Establishment.

In 1966, Warner Brothers released a tremendously popular film version of the play, filmed at Smith College, starring Elizabeth Taylor and Richard Burton. (Leslie Weiner, W. A. Storrer, T. C. Johnson, and Leonard J. Leff each provide insights on the correspondence of the play to the screen version.) A success both critically and financially, the film only increased the public's awareness of Albee's masterwork. Newspapers nationwide reported the explosive response the public had toward the play. Censored, altered, labeled "for adults only," even banned in certain cities, the play's language and exhausting character clashes made Albee the center of one conflict after another.

THE SCHOLARLY RESPONSE

If a play attracts, as Jonas Barish writes apropos Shakespeare studies, "unwelcome surgery" that scholars inflict on a text,[18] there is nonetheless an abundance of exemplary criticism available on *Who's Afraid of Virginia Woolf?*. The scholarly works present a more thoughtful, if no less diverse, assessment than the reviewers' more hastily composed judgments.

Almost all cite Albee's technical virtuosity as embedded in his language. He animates his theater through language. Indeed, language stands as the most delightful feature of his dramaturgy as well as his major contribution to American drama. In both text and performance, Albee captures the values, personal politics, and perceptions of his characters through language. He "revolutionized the language of the American stage, extending verbal metaphor into the visual settings of his plays, working isolated ironic meanings into a complex network of interrelated ironic reverberations, and using epic topography to maintain allegorical simplicity," writes Anne Paolucci in her influential *From Tension to Tonic: The Plays of Edward Albee*.[19] Ruby Cohn praises the play's witty dialogue,[20] and in his *A Critical Introduction to Twentieth-Century American Drama*, C. W. E. Bigsby notes Albee's language for its rhythms and nuances.[21] Although the language from *A Delicate Balance* onward becomes, as Thomas P. Adler argues, more stylized, elliptical, even "pretentious and obscure,"[22] Albee's repartee in his masterwork sparkles.

Many view the play as a model of sociopolitical protest. Michael E. Rutenberg in *Edward Albee: Playwright in Protest* investigates exactly this aspect of the play, a critical perspective on which A. D. Choudhuri, in *The Face of Illusion in American Drama*, elaborates. Choudhuri sees the play as an attack on American culture and a lament for a pervading sterility that neutralizes human relationships. More recently Gerry McCarthy also concentrates on the ideological dimensions of the play, particularly from a performance (rather than textual) vantage point.

Others enjoy identifying in the play traces of absurdist theater. Taking as a point of departure Martin Esslin's *The Theatre of the Absurd*, Elizabeth Phillips, L. Howard Quackenbush, and Brian Way provide differing, and sensible, discussions of the play's absurdist affinities. Clearly the play is not an absurdist work in the tradition of Beckett, Adamov, Genet, and Ionesco, nor is it really like Albee's own contribution to the absurdist canon, *The American Dream*. However, as Elemér Hankiss and

Wendell V. Harris argue, the play has its absurdist moments, as when George quickly invents the fiction within a fiction—that he just ate the telegram bearing news of their son's death—but that, unlike so many absurdist dramas, *Who's Afraid of Virginia Woolf?* outlines, however vaguely, the possibility of free choice and hope.

Countless others have concentrated on the epistemological tensions established through the truth and illusion matrix within the play. Ruth Meyer analyzes the ways in which the characters' perceptions, filtered through their own distorted lenses, mediate between various levels of truth and debilitating illusions; the characters' perceptions, in turn, allow the audience to blend traditional appearance/reality dualities. Thomas P. Adler also perceptively treats the subject, but through a thoughtful character examination observes that the banishment of the illusion is the first step toward spiritual regeneration.

Joy Flasch and Louis Paul point out the ways in which the play reflects the pragmatics of human intercourse, especially in relation to Eric Berne's *Games People Play,* which was published two years after *Who's Afraid of Virginia Woolf?*. Similarly, Paul Watzawick holds the play up as a perfect case study for psychologists because it highlights, in clinical parlance, a communicational approach to interactional human encounters. Indeed, scholars have had a field day with the role of communication in the play, for throughout his theater Albee highlights the primacy of communication to such an extent that most critics see "communication" as one of the hallmarks of his canon.

The five collections of critical essays now available on Albee also reflect the enormous variety of critical methodologies exacted on the play. In 1975 Bigsby edited a provocative volume, *Edward Albee: A Collection of Critical Essays,* and in the following years, four other edited collections were published: *Edward Albee: Planned Wilderness,* by Patricia De La Fuente; *Edward Albee: An Interview and Essays,* by Julian N. Wasserman; *Critical Essays on Edward Albee,* by Philip C. Kolin and J. Madison Davis; and *Edward Albee: Modern Critical Views,* by Harold Bloom. All are extremely helpful, although the Kolin-Davis volume, with thirty-nine essays, stands out as the exemplary collection. Within these volumes scholars identify other key motifs, themes, and influences embedded in *Who's Afraid of Virginia Woolf?*, qualities that have since come to characterize vintage Albee. The necessity of ritualized tyranny and confrontation, the paradoxical mixture of love and hate, the cleverly abrasive dialogue, the religious overtones, the ideological fields of references, the tragic force of abandonment and death, the awareness of a gulf between the way things are versus the way things could be, and the penalty of consciousness all manifest themselves in Albee's most dynamic composition.

Perhaps the most hotly debated issue concerns the son-myth and the attendant exorcism. Three decades of critical exegesis may be roughly divided into two schools of thought regarding this issue: those who feel that the son-myth and exorcism fail and are much ado about little, and those who see in the play's ending a purgative, cleansing process that is both structurally and thematically decorous. In his *The Theater of Protest and Paradox*, for instance, George Wellwarth essentially agrees with Brustein's view that the son-myth seems unconvincing, contending that "there is nothing more in this than a dissection of an extremely ambiguously conceived sick marriage. In writing *Who's Afraid of Virginia Woolf?* Albee looks like a man expending a tremendous amount of energy on furiously pedaling backwards."[23] Others find the son-myth so feeble that it is like tracing the source of Niagara Falls to a water gun, and Harold Bloom thinks that George and Martha are reduced to blathering fools after the exorcism. More positive readings of the son-myth abound. "Exposure of the [son] myth—it could concern God and America as well as the imaginary son of George and Martha—opens the way for harrowing reconciliations," explains Ihab Hassan,[24] a point developed by Bigsby, Anita Maria Stenz, and Gerry McCarthy. After a sensitive and convincing discussion of the illusion and ending, Paolucci, I think, places the son-myth and exorcism in perspective when she explains, "In *Who's Afraid of Virginia Woolf?*, the existential dilemma is dramatized with full sympathy in its most painful human immediacy. The weak are redeemed in their helplessness, and the vicious are forgiven in their tortured self-awareness."[25] Although scholars establish many distinctions relative to the degree of artistic success ascribed to the son-myth and exorcism, nearly all the authors of the (at last count) fourteen book-length studies on Albee address the idea of the possibility of redemption as engendered in the son-myth and exorcism.

Several of the many books devoted to Albee deserve mention for their quality of thought. Debusscher's *Edward Albee: Tradition and Renewal* places Albee in a useful historical context, citing him as the American dramatist most worthy of carrying on the legacies of O'Neill, Miller, and Williams. With his masterwork, Albee gave "the American stage its first great work in years." According to Debusscher, Albee assimilated rather than copied the French avant-garde styles in the early plays but produced a distinctly American cadence. Debusscher claims that Albee is technically sound but often lapses into " 'theater for theater's sake.' " He provides a sensible reading of *Who's Afraid of Virginia Woolf?*, but concludes that Albee is a nihilist: "Albee's work contains no positive philosophical or social message. His theatre belongs in the pessimistic, defeatist or nihilistic current which characterizes the entire contemporary theatrical scene."[26] Subsequent studies would build upon, and challenge, Debusscher's conclusions.

Four studies on Albee appeared in 1969, and C. W. E. Bigsby's remains the best. His *Albee* locates Albee's impulse to dramatize man's need "to break out of his self-imposed isolation" and establish "contact with his fellow man," to experience a "revival of love." Despite his social protests, Albee's interest lies in a more "fundamental sense of alienation," and in exploring the "source of a limited but genuine hope" in human encounters.[27]

Ruby Cohn's pamphlet, *Edward Albee*, is a brief but substantive study of Albee. For Cohn, Albee is obsessed with stripping away illusions within human experience: "Whereas Sartre, Camus, Beckett, Genet, Ionesco, and Pinter represent that reality in all its alogical absurdity, Albee has been preoccupied with illusions that screen man from reality."[28] Cohn, like Debusscher and Bigsby, brings an international perspective to our understanding of Albee's language and theatrics, and opens the way for an important study that would come three years later—Paolucci's.

From Tension to Tonic: The Plays of Edward Albee, Paolucci's provocative 1972 book, rivals Bigsby's work in its analytical rigor and critical insights. For Paolucci, "Albee is the only playwright, after O'Neill, who shows real growth, the only one who has made serious effort to break away from the 'message' plays which have plagued our theater since O'Neill. Experimentation, for Albee, is a slow internal transformation of the dramatic medium . . . His arrogance is not an empty gesture. He is the only one of our playwrights who seems to have accepted and committed himself to serious articulation of the existential questions of our time, recognizing the incongruity of insisting on pragmatic values in an age of relativity."[29] Paolucci covers the plays through *Box-Mao-Box,* and remains essential reading for Albee scholars.

Anita Maria Stenz's *Edward Albee: The Poet of Loss,* a solid psychological reading of characters, discusses the plays through *Seascape.* She concludes: "In all of Albee's plays the moral imperative is the obligation for everyone to live with awareness. The demands of institutions and the barriers people build around themselves prevent them from seeing the realities of their condition and foster the creation of self-destructive illusions." And here Stenz makes the important distinction that informs her reading of George and Martha: "Albee does not damn an institution in itself but insists that its demands should not override the natural human need for self-development and constructive relationships with other people."[30]

Finally, Bigsby returns to Albee in his authoritative *A Critical Introduction to Twentieth-Century American Drama,* which is essential reading. He relies extensively on Albee's unpublished materials, and his sense of social history and existentialism enhances his illuminating study. Albee has tackled, concludes Bigsby, "issues of genuine metaphysical seriousness in a way that few American dramatists before him have claimed to do, and done so, for the most part, with a command of wit and a controlled humour which has not always characterized the work of O'Neill, Miller and Williams. He has set himself the task of probing beneath the bland surface of contemporary reality and created a theatre which at its best is luminous with intelligence and power." The critical and popular success of *Who's Afraid of Virginia Woolf?* "consolidated Albee's reputation. The first of his generation successfully to accomplish the transition from Off-Broadway to Broadway, he did so without making any concessions . . . to that audience's supposed sensibility. Twenty years later the play still holds up and has deservedly come to be regarded as one of the classics of the American stage."[31] Simply put, Bigsby's books on Albee are the best we have.[32]

A READING

4

Introduction: Toward the Marrow

Love had a thousand shapes. There might be lovers whose gift it was to choose out the elements of things and place them together and so, giving them a wholeness not theirs in life, make of some scene, or meeting of people (all now gone and separate), one of those globed compacted things over which thought lingers, and love plays.
—Virginia Woolf, *To the Lighthouse*

Who's Afraid of Virginia Woolf? is Albee's most affirmative work. Many considering the play for the first time may find such a claim untenable, but beneath the playfully devastating gamesmanship and overt animosity lies the animating principle of genuine love which—sometimes unspeakably, always paradoxically—unites its players. Near the end of *Who's Afraid of Virginia Woolf?* George explains to a mesmerized Honey, "When you get down to bone, you haven't got all the way, yet. There's something inside the bone . . . the marrow . . . and that's what you gotta get at. (*A strange smile at Martha*)" (213). The reference to the "marrow" is vital. The "marrow" allusion provides a key dramatic moment in the action, a controlled emotional high point for George, a telling emotional still point for the audience. For at this moment George finally realizes what needs to be done to save, not his marriage, but his and Martha's very existence: the son-myth crippling their world must be confronted and, against unfavorable odds, purged from their psyche. The "marrow" allusion signifies George's awareness that stripping away the illusion governing their lives is necessary for survival. Such knowledge prepares the audience for the particular intensity and ambivalent resolutions established after three-and-one-half hours of bloodletting. George finally

29

realizes that to excise the incubi haunting their psyches he must first emotionally prepare Martha for "total war" (159) by externalizing the child-myth, which symbolically places us in the "marrow" or the essence of their relationship. Catharsis precedes spiritual regeneration.

Curiously enough, the very exorcising process that liberates George and Martha prompts many critics to fault the play's ending. Too sentimental, too indeterminate, the play's resolution for many produces hollow resonances. The exorcising of the son-myth is not plausible psychologically, and the tenuous reunion of George and Martha appears unacceptably saccharine, somehow unearned. The tremendous emotional tension Albee works so carefully to objectify, other critics feel, collapses miserably from its own weight: the killing of the child and denouement simply do not account for all the evening's dizzying events. "Coming after two acts of cascading turbulence," writes one reviewer, "this plot resolution is woefully inadequate and incongruous, rather like tracing the source of Niagara to a water pistol."[1] Shorn of their private fantasy, George and Martha emerge more as two infantile adults recovering from an evening of self-generated hysteria rather than as caring or conscious individuals. They survive, for Harold Bloom, "only to endure the endless repetition of drowning their breaths, in this harsh world, in order to go on telling our story." Citing what he and others pinpoint as Albee's decline in powers of mimetic representation, Bloom consigns George and Martha to caricature types and the play as "a drama of impaling, of love gone rancid because of a metaphysical lack." After their exorcism, Bloom thinks, George and Martha reduce themselves to near nothingness. "George talks, ineffectually; Martha brays, ineffectually; that is their initial reality, when we come upon them. Martha barely talks, or is silent; George is almost equally monosyllabic, when we leave them. A silent or monosyllabic ineffectuality has replaced chattering and braying, both ineffectual. Nothing has happened, because nothing has changed, and so this couple will be rubbed down to rubbish in the end."[2]

Such a reading misses the point, however. Rather than appearing grossly oversimplified or emotionally unjustified, the ending appears more convincing when we see that it stages the re-visioning process Albee insists is necessary for his characters' spiritual aliveness. The

Introduction: Toward the Marrow

schisms and asymmetries between George and Martha give way to rapprochement, rapprochement to relationship, and relationship to love.
The threat of anomie yields to the hope of authentic engagement. The
stage directions are important in the closing moments; there is a *"hint of
communion"* (238) in their quiet exchange. Gone are the rhetorical gal-
lantries. These two connoisseurs of verbal dueling now communicate
simply, directly, with no wasted emotion. Once so ennobled by their
lexical inventiveness, conferring upon an illusion the status of objective
reality, George and Martha are brought to earth, not merely by sacrificing their son, but also by sacrificing the very language which defined
their moral imagination. The game-playing, for now, is all over. In place
of embellished repartee we hear a disjointed, splintered exchange, a
duologue whose tonal quality emphasizes their frightening reentry into
the here and now—and into reality. Just as Virginia Woolf in the third
section of *To the Lighthouse* presents Lily asking a series of necessary
questions, so Albee in the third act presents Martha asking vital questions that hint at images of unity and resolutions, however tentative,
that manifest themselves. The halting speech patterns, invested with
tenderness and felt love, confirm George and Martha's collective willingness to face their inadequacies honestly:

> *Martha:* It was . . . ? You had to?
>
> *George:* (*Pause*) Yes.
>
> *Martha:* I don't know.
>
> *George:* It was . . . time.
>
> *Martha:* Was it?
>
> *George:* Yes.
>
> *Martha:* (*Pause*) I'm cold.
>
> *George:* It's late.
>
> *Martha:* Yes.
>
> *George:* (*Long silence*) It will be better.
>
> *Martha:* (*Long silence*) I don't . . . know.
>
> *George:* It will be . . . maybe.
>
> *Martha:* I'm . . . not . . . sure.

31

George: No.

Martha: Just ... us?

George: Yes.

Martha: I don't suppose, maybe, we could ...

George: No, Martha.

Martha: Yes. No.

George: Are you all right?

Martha: Yes. No.

George: (*Puts his hand gently on her shoulder; she puts her head back and he sings to her, very softly*):
Who's afraid of Virginia Woolf,
    Virginia Woolf,
    Virginia Woolf,

Martha: I ... am ... George....

George: Who's afraid of Virginia Woolf....

Martha: I ... am ... George.... I ... am...
(George *nods, slowly*)
(*Silence; tableau*) (240–42)

The minimalist scene is important. Albee deliberately reduces, deflates the mystical encounter, his technique for spotlighting his heroes' inclination to repair the ruins of their past by confronting the present unfettered by any illusions. Structurally, the scene parallels the opening moments of the play with Martha's repeated question-asking. Whereas the opening questions were laced with sarcasm, gamesmanship, and anger, however, the closing inquiries are free from the nervousness, the incredible tensions. Earlier George and Martha reveled in questions that deliberately maimed. They are now more willing to ask difficult questions geared toward restoring order and marriage. Anxiety and fear remain; but relationship replaces hatred, love overrides indifference. The very tone and language of their closing exchanges suggest their resolution and willingness, not to return to "sanity" or "happiness," but to begin the messy and complex process, however unpredictable, of confronting their essential selves honestly—one step at a time. The scene signals the end of their fantasy, the compression of words underscoring their newfound perception. Before, they were capable of elevating an illusion constructed and sustained by words to the status of objective reality. Now the very nature of those words is markedly different: where once the vacant spaces were masked with a marvelously devastating language-war, now those vacancies are granted their presence, as insecurities are no longer concealed with linguistic ambushes. C. W. E. Bigsby pinpoints exactly Albee's achievement: "The play ends with a radically simplified language, with a simple cadence of monosyllabic question and answer. Language no longer comes between them. Neither does illusion. The fabric of their fiction has come apart. They are left only with one another, with relationship; they acknowledge the responsibility which they had previously evaded."[3] Personal inadequacies are now as fully accepted as they were once denied and then later exposed.

The play's closure affirms what Jerry in *The Zoo Story* discovered: "sometimes a person has to go a very long distance out of his way to come back a short distance correctly" (*ZS*, 21). The ending of *Who's Afraid of Virginia Woolf?* heralds (in muted tones) the first step in living, in Jerry's word, "correctly." Albee resists, I think, oversentimentalizing the ending by placing a premium on indeterminacy and inconclusiveness. The son-illusion defleshed, George and Martha confront the terror in the actual, accepting their existence shorn of the devitalizing-though-once-comforting myth that has governed, and confined, their world. Albee provides no social constructs guaranteeing order, comprehension, or survival. Ambivalences prevail. And this is precisely why the play's resolution succeeds in dramatic and thematic terms: Albee concedes that the ever-real presence of human fallibility, mutability, the potency of self-annihilating myths lurk, perhaps subconsciously, as destructive temptations. This explains the playwright's comment on O'Neill. *Who's Afraid of Virginia Woolf?*, Albee has said, stands as a response to *The Iceman Cometh*, a response acknowledging that the abrogation of the self, of the will to being, is but a drink or a fiction away. For O'Neill's heroes, illusions help; for Albee's, they destroy. Within *Who's Afraid of Virginia Woolf?*, as repressed feelings give way to honest admissions, so denial gives way to acceptance.

A unique feature of the play's ending, then, concerns the resilience of George and Martha's collective imagination to reconstruct reality by subordinating illusion to truth. Theirs is a recognition of the regenerative powers implicit in facing human existence without what Henrik Ibsen in *The Wild Duck* coined "life-lies." Albee enjoys referring to the affirmative texture of his masterpiece, and it is the plot resolution that embodies such affirmation. The ending defines what Albee would later call "the cleansing consciousness of death" (*TP*, 10). The play challenges, Albee tells us, the sorts of illusions paralyzing the figures in *The Iceman Cometh*. "It's about going against the 'pipe-dreams.' After all, *Who's Afraid of Virginia Woolf?* just says have your pipe-dreams if you want to but realize you are kidding yourself."[4]

But Albee quickly ups the stakes of the game; the play's three-act structure chronicles George and Martha's realization that their "pipe-dream," their imaginary son, is "kidding" as well as killing them. Such recognition, though, comes only after two decades of fabricating and nurturing their child-illusion. Private mythology turns to public issue, however, early in act 1, Martha's casual off-stage remarks to Honey about her son signaling an ominous shift in the marriage relationship and the psychodynamics of the games they play. Albee establishes the importance of Martha's revelation, not only through dialogue, but through George's non-verbal response:

> Honey: (*To George, brightly*) I didn't know until just a minute ago that you had a *son*.
>
> George: (*Wheeling, as if struck from behind*) WHAT? (44)

The private game now jars the public facade: revelation of the son-myth violates George and Martha's pledge of discretion relative to their fantasy world.

5

WHO'S AFRAID OF WHAT?
ALBEE'S STRATEGY

Albee's technical strategy involves deliberately leading the audience into a series of unknowns. Albee decenters the audience. He creates a sense of mystery regarding their son, for George and Martha will continually allude to their child, but always obliquely, and always with a felt nervous tension. Not until the exorcism will the audience, with Nick and Honey, realize that the son is a fiction. Further, the intensity of George's question to Honey suggests the seriousness of Martha's slip, a violation of their lifelong agreement never publicly to "start in on the bit about the kid" (18). That Honey, an *outsider*, suddenly possesses knowledge of their innermost creation certifies the enormity of their illusion. What originally started out as mere game playing, the lovers' fanciful procreation of a symbolic child they could never have, has grown into a bizarre relationship on the verge of exploding from its own neuroses. By breaking the unwritten laws of the game, Martha unwittingly forces a definitive confrontation regarding their grasp on objective reality. More than a social embarrassment—after all, what's so unusual about mentioning one's child?—Martha's publicizing their son's existence signals, George recognizes, that their private life has disintegrated into an unreal, terrifying make-believe world. Distinctions between truth and illusion become blurred, not by the continual drinking, but by an overwhelming psychotic reliance on fiction as truth. George's refrain—"Truth and illusion. Who knows the difference, eh, toots? Eh?" (201)—becomes a disarming refrain, a haunting monody throughout the play. More than mere witticisms, his numerous truth and illusion references shape some of the epistemological dimensions of the play. This thematic concern of Albee's will become increasingly pronounced in subsequent plays, especially *Tiny Alice* (1964), *Quotations from Chairman Mao Tse-Tung* (1968), and *The Lady from Dubuque* (1980). The truth and illusion refrain also testifies to George's awareness of and commitment to sorting through the real and the imaginary, and places his cruel verbal attacks in a broader context. George confirms the point when the comic outburst transforms into the tragic insight:

> But you've taken a new tack, Martha, over the past couple of centuries—or however long it's been I've lived in this house with you— that makes it just too much . . . too much. I don't mind your dirty underthings in public . . . well, I *do* mind, but I've reconciled myself to that . . . but you've moved bag and baggage into your own fantasy world now, and you've started playing variations on your own distortions, and, as a result . . . . (155)

This moment crystallizes the dangers of their games and is as revealing to George as it is vital to Martha. As if coming out of a years-long drunken stupor, George gradually realizes, as booze and compromise give way to sober insight and thought, that he must shock Martha into some definitive awareness of her deteriorating state. George, like Albee himself, must become the anger artist. His lines taper off in the passage above, but the suggestion is clear: Martha, and probably George, will descend deeper into their own form of madness if they do not relinquish their dependency on such "distortions."

6

MADNESS

Madness pervades *Who's Afraid of Virginia Woolf?*. Albee has always demonstrated a fascination with exploring the darker side of the human soulscape, and the various guises madness assumes within human encounters. Albee has said that his plays concern "imbalance" and "people out of kilter," and that his task as an artist is to "represent what the imbalances are."[1] Hence Jerry in *The Zoo Story* (1959) has an almost Hamlet-like quality about his ravings, Julian in *Tiny Alice* (1964) confesses that he was once institutionalized, and Agnes in *A Delicate Balance* (1966) openly worries about being possessed by demons. Madness manifests itself in selected later plays as well—the disturbed young woman in *Listening* (1976) slits her wrists, and the protagonist in *The Man Who Had Three Arms* (1987) appears nearly insane throughout the entire play.

Anger in *Who's Afraid of Virginia Woolf?* is obvious. Madness seems concealed. Madness never reaches the tragic proportions witnessed in, say, *The Zoo Story*; never captures the heroic extremes of, say, *Hamlet*. Rather, Albee infuses madness into the everyday realism of the play's action and language, resulting in a gradual stripping away of structures of order, the façade of rationality. Whereas in many of his other works he rather overtly stages madness, in *Who's Afraid of Virginia*

Woolf? Albee muffles, even camouflages madness. By act 2 we have a full sense of the characters' anger; but only in act 3 do we fully comprehend the extent of George and Martha's psychic dislocation. Albee never talks about the madness; the process is strictly dramatic, revealed gradually and only through the artistry itself. The aggressively militant script shrouds George and Martha's insanity until the end, when the audience, too, shares in the shock of recognition. The audience becomes so involved in the action that the mysteriousness of the seemingly realistic set and dialogue covers the madness, masks the psychological hemorrhaging. What originally seems closer to anger and frustration shifts into a broader, more disarming range of human emotions.

Paradoxically, on one level their madness preserves their supposed sense of coherence and lucidity. Madness, for George and Martha, sanctions the birth and growth of the child, and provides the appropriate rationalizations needed to sustain the myth. And, indeed, for years the child has fulfilled the couple. "He walked evenly between us," Martha says, "a hand out to each of us for what we could offer by way of support, affection, teaching, even love" (221). Illusions, denials, and self-betrayals are the things used to reconstitute their previously arid world.

On another level, however, the severity of their madness intensifies. Each act reflects the change, the play's structure mirroring the building intensity. The "Fun and Games" of act 1 build to the Walpurgisnacht of act 2, and reaches a crescendo and coda in the "Exorcism" of act 3. As the pressure of their myth reaches its critical mass, as rational analysis sparks additional marital skirmishes, George knows that they are at a Sophoclean crossroad, a crux moment in which the past, recollected in hostility, forces a calling of the question. Both George and Martha are not only at a turning point but a breaking point. They have crossed an imaginary threshold, approaching what Saul Bellow calls "the borders of sense," the place where the powers of mystery override the rational faculties. The witches released in Walpurgisnacht dominate. As Oedipus finally accepted his tragic fate, so George accepts his, discovering too the full nature of his sin: the collusion; the disintegration of the self; the abrogation of responsibility; the surrender of the spirit. George's self-scrutiny is not designed to match or somehow mirror the tragic fury that

Oedipus' generated; Sophocles conceived his play in macrocosmic terms. Though scaled down, Albee's play nonetheless evokes a sense of an apocalyptic vision. George's willingness to investigate, to adopt a truth-at-all-costs stance toward cleansing his and Martha's souls evokes, in the Aristotelian sense, pity, fear, and admiration.

George recognizes that as he moves closer to self-identification, another set of possibilities suggest themselves. He is not only a player-in-the-games but the author of the very rules of those games. "We are going on," he declares as an aroused, angry director, "and I'm going to have at you, and it's going to make your performance tonight look like an Easter pageant" (208). Viewed as a metatheatrical character, as June Schlueter argues in *Metafictional Characters in Modern Drama*, George moves simultaneously from the consummate player of roles to the scripter of such roles, the director of the action, the producer of spectacle. Above all, George *performs*. He first appears as the external observer of Martha's condition and then suddenly becomes an internal participant, a co-conspirator with Martha in their shared fantasies. *Who's Afraid of Virginia Woolf?* thus can be viewed as a Pirandellian work: a play whose words, gestures, and epistemological questions transform much of the action—despite its ostensibly realistic medium—into what Lionel Abel would call a metatheatrical experience. At times the play calls attention to its artificiality, deliberately making the spectator aware of the theatricality of the play. In the following exchange, for instance, George and Martha know that they are entertaining, acting, even using their guests for their own theatrical purposes. Here George deliberately ignores Martha while she desperately tries to gain his attention:

> George: (*Never looking up*) No, no, now . . . you go right ahead . . . you entertain your guests.
>
> Martha: I'm going to entertain myself, too.
>
> George: Good . . . good.
>
> Martha: Ha, ha. You're a riot, George.
>
> George: Unh-hunh.
>
> Martha: Well, I'm a riot, too, George.

George: Yes you are, Martha.

(*Nick takes Martha's hand, pulls her to him. They stop for a moment, then kiss, not briefly*)

Martha: (*After*) You know what I'm doing, George?

George: No, Martha . . . what are you doing?

Martha: I'm entertaining. I'm entertaining one of the guests. I'm necking with one of the guests.

George: (*Seemingly relaxed and preoccupied, never looking*) Oh, that's nice. Which one? (170)

Other times the play calls attention to its own language while at the same time exposing the pure gamesmanship of that language. At times George and Martha know that they are performers performing before an audience within an audience—Nick and Honey as well as the actual theatergoer—as the following spontaneous exchange suggests:

Martha: (*To Nick*) We're sitting up . . . we're having coffee, and we'll be back in.

Nick: (*Not rising*) Oh . . . is there anything I should do?

Martha: Nayh. You just stay here and listen to George's side of things. Bore yourself to death.

George: Monstre!

Martha: Cochon!

George: Bête!

Martha: Canaille!

George: Putain!

Martha: (*With a gesture of contemptuous dismissal*) Yaaaahhhh! You two types amuse yourselves . . . we'll be in. (*As she goes*) You clean up the mess you made, George? (101)

In a sense, characters almost become different people. Like Pirandello, Genet, and Beckett before him, Albee at times embellishes scenes with a deliberate self-consciousness, calling attention to the play as artifice.

Albee's Pirandellian touches function on at least two important levels. First, such a technique invites the audience to question its willing suspension of disbelief. By calling attention to the very nature of theatricality, Albee experiments with the illusion of dramatic mimesis, challenging traditional responses to the theater. *Who's Afraid of Virginia Woolf?* suggests that, with his first foray into the world of Broadway, Albee was willing, indeed, eager to take aesthetic risks, to bedevil more conservative audiences with the daring experimentalism that characterized much of contemporary European drama. (Soon after the play opened, Albee charged that "Broadway audiences are such placid cows" [*CEA*, 22], although his masterwork succeeded in arousing even the more orthodox audiences.) Second, like Pirandello's *Six Characters in Search of an Author, Who's Afraid of Virginia Woolf?* invites the audience to break down, or at least minimize, the barrier between itself and the actors, thus creating a more intimate, and dangerous, theater experience. The emotional effect is to involve the audience directly, as participants in the action. "Think about it," Albee observed in 1971. "What really happened in *Virginia Woolf?* All the action took place in the *spectator*" (*CEA*, 104). Despite the proscenium arch, and despite what emerges as the play's blatant theatricalism, Albee's dialogue creates an uneasy intimacy between actor and spectator. It is a case of the "watchers watching the watchers watch," to use Blau's words.[2] This is a play about those seeing and those seen. Albee does not direct George and Martha to fight with the actual audience, as Julian Beck had members of *The Living Theatre* do with his audience. Still, he scripts an overly aggressive text, expanding the boundaries of theater as collective, communal spectacle. Albee discussed this point two decades after his masterwork, observing the relatedness of the actors and audience within his theory of drama:

> In nine or ten of my plays, you'll notice, actors talk directly to the audience. In my mind, this is a way of involving the audience; of embarrassing, if need be, the audience into participation. It may have a reverse effect: some audiences don't like this; they get upset by it quite often; it may alienate them. But I am trying very hard to *involve* them. I don't like the audience as voyeur, the audience as passive spectator. I want the audience as participant. In that sense, I agree with Artaud: that sometimes we should literally draw blood. I am very fond of doing that because voyeurism in the theater lets people off the hook.[3]

With its relentless verbal dueling, *Who's Afraid of Virginia Woolf?* draws "blood," directly involving the audience in its calculated violence. George and Martha put into concrete voice Albee's Artaudian dramatic theory. Albee may be regarded as a leading proponent of using cruelty as a method of purging oneself of demons, of effecting a sense of catharsis, factors which seem germane to Artaud's Theater of Cruelty.

Equally important to Artaud was the magical and transcendent quality that theater, by nature of the genre itself, possesses. By probing into primal, archetypal realities, Artaud theorized, the producer and playwright could release repressed desires buried within the subconscious by outward societal norms and mores. The implicit miraculism of live theater could liberate, Artaud felt, and these ideas clearly exert a tremendous influence on Albee's dramatic conception. So Artaud casts an important shadow for Albee, and we will return to his influence presently.

Within Albee's Artaudian method, then, George blatantly calls attention to the theatricality of his own theater: the parasol as gun scene; the games he orchestrates ("Hump the Hostess," "Get the Guests"); of course the entire exorcism process ("Bringing Up Baby"), in which he becomes nothing less than metaphysical surgeon and high priest; and then the decrescendo, the final moments in which George and Martha are merely themselves. So the interplay of truth and illusion, the subversive influence of the text on the stage action, the attendant effect of minimizing the actor/audience barrier—these are the sorts of dramatic innovations Luigi Chiarelli, Luigi Pirandello, and Michel de Ghelderode pioneered and which, in *Who's Afraid of Virginia Woolf?*, Albee selectively employs. (Such experiments with the ontological status of the theater are particularly evident in such Albee plays as *Fam and Yam* [1960], *The Sandbox* [1960], *The American Dream* [1960], *The Lady from Dubuque* [1980], and *The Man Who Had Three Arms* [1987].)

From early in act 1 onward, most of George's social and psychological strategies center on one goal: exorcising the son-illusion distorting (and perverting) their lives. George and Martha, Schlueter points out, lead dual existences, their real identities as characters in a play intermingling with their fictive identities as parents of a fantasy child. "While Martha is thoroughly involved emotionally with their creation,"

Madness

Schlueter suggests, "George, as artist-director, maintains a distance from the boy, using him as a means of pandering to Martha's frustrations and gaining control over a woman who by nature is the stronger force in their marriage. Following each emotional involvement which George as character experiences, George as artist-director grabs hold of the strings that control him and Martha."[4] Within this context George and Martha's brutalizing language, which escalates with each act, becomes a necessary social and psychological dynamic. In other words, the final expiation of the illusion is made possible by externalizing the lies governing their, and Nick and Honey's, relationship through such games as "Hump the Hostess," "Get the Guests," and, finally, "Bringing Up Baby." Conflict precedes resolution.

Although *Who's Afraid of Virginia Woolf?* stages a battle between the sexes, Albee's ultimate interest lies in presenting love as a unifying presence. Albee supplants the lack of compassion in *The Death of Bessie Smith* and the apathy in *The American Dream* with George and Martha's reciprocal care and love. Love's opposite—indifference—finds no place in their marriage. Albee's dialogue mixes kindness and cruelty, what Jerry in *The Zoo Story* confesses is an unforgettable "teaching emotion," making George and Martha's verbal clashes, for better or worse, an ineluctable element of their relationship. Therefore, George can accurately describe his wife as a "spoiled, self-indulgent, willful, dirty-minded, liquor-ridden" woman (157), and Martha, with equal accuracy, may counter with verbal salvos, as when she attacks his professional shortcomings: "You see, George didn't have much . . . push . . . he wasn't particularly . . . aggressive. In fact he was sort of a . . . (*Spits the word at George's back*) . . . A FLOP! A great . . . big . . . fat . . . FLOP!" (84). They are duelists who plainly thrive off of individual and collective wizardry, shrewdness, and cleverness. But their wittily devastating repartee is born out of a profound love for the other, a point they lose sight of but regain in act 3. Hate precedes the restoration of love.

7

WHO'S AFRAID OF EDWARD ALBEE?

Before turning to the play in more detail, perhaps we can better come to terms with its militant action by considering Albee's dramatic theory and art. After Jerry astonished audiences by impaling himself on the knife in *The Zoo Story* and Grandma recounted with appalling specificity the spiritual dismemberment of the child in *The American Dream*, Edward Albee became well-known for his dramatization of fatal attractions. Verbal challenges, social confrontations, sudden deaths—real and fictional, physical and psychological—permeate the Albee canon. His plays typically address such issues as betrayal, abandonment, sexual tension, the primacy of communication, loss of personal ambition, withdrawal into a death-in-life existence—hardly issues appealing to the entertainment-oriented taste of Broadway. Still, with *Who's Afraid of Virginia Woolf?*, as with his other works, Albee did not compromise artistic instinct and theatrical integrity for box office sales pressures.

The Albee hero and the Albee text, with disarming consistency, seem almost savagely divided against themselves. Given the militancy of his scripts and the preponderance of self-devouring characters, it is hardly surprising to find students, reviewers, and critics pigeonholing Albee as a pessimistic or even nihilistic writer, a dramatist whose plays are singlemindedly fixed on staging the demonic, the destructive. To be sure, Albee is a writer whose moral seriousness and belief in the purgative influence of confrontation and death leave him open to charges of cynicism, defeatism, and nihilism.

As a play that sparkles as it puzzles, one that invites, and absorbs, a multitude of "interpretations" while simultaneously appearing naturally resistant to scholarly discourse, *Who's Afraid of Virginia Woolf?* may be viewed from a variety of critical perspectives without depleting its artistic resources and "meanings." One way to understand the play more fully, however, is to consider Albee's moral and aesthetic preoccupations.

Albee's world view presupposes the talismanic powers of the theater to trigger public awareness and private insight. Or at least he enjoys staging the *possibility,* however such possibility may be vitiated by external forces, that his play can ask the audience to see and be seen with, as Bellow says, "the awakened eye of the spirit." This notion, I think, underpins all of Albee's performative theories. It is very possible to locate in all the plays an affirmative vision of human experience, one dispelling, or at least greatly minimizing, Albee's reputation as a nihilist. Such an affirmative stance takes on compelling vividness in *Who's Afraid of Virginia Woolf?*

Underneath the external action and obvious concern with death lies an inner drama, one disclosing the playwright's *compassion* for his fellow human being. This sense of compassion, this affirmative vision, becomes easier to understand when we listen to the playwright. Albee, himself, outlines what thematically engages his imagination:

> I am very concerned with the fact that so many people turn off because it is easier; that they don't stay fully aware during the course of their lives, in all the choices they make: social, economic, political, aesthetic. They turn off because it's easier. But I find that anything less than absolutely full, dangerous participation is an absolute waste of some rather valuable time. . . . I am concerned with being as self-aware, and open to all kinds of experience on its own terms—I think those conditions, given half a chance, will produce better self-government, a better society, a better everything else.[1]

Albee's observations provide a key to understanding all of the plays. Alluding to a spiritual malaise that may psychologically anesthetize the individual, Albee suggests that "full, dangerous participation" in human intercourse is a necessary correlate to living authentically. His remarks also suggest his underlying hope or optimism for his fellow human being. Albee agrees with Martin Heidegger in *Being and Time* that through the process of existing itself, the individual may sculpt a "better self-government." The Albee play, we see, becomes equipment for living. As the Girl in Albee's *Listening* recalls, "'We do not have to live, you know, unless we wish to; the greatest sin, no matter what they *tell* you, the greatest sin in living is doing it badly—stupidly, as if you weren't really alive'" (*L*, 110). In plays as different in dramatic conception as *The Zoo Story, Finding the Sun* (1983), *Walking* (1984), or *Marriage Play* (1987), Albee consistently implies that one can choose consciously to mix the intellect and the emotion into a new whole, measured qualitatively, which is the aware individual.

A technically versatile dramatist, Albee demonstrates—often at the cost of commercial, if not critical, success—a willingness to take aesthetic risks, a deliberate attempt to explore the ontological status of theatricality itself. As Albee writes in his prefatory remarks to *Box* and *Quotations From Chairman Mao Tse-Tung* (both 1968), two of his most structurally experimental plays, "Since art must move, or wither—the playwright must try to alter the forms within which his precursors have had to work" (*BQ*, x). Each play demonstrates Albee's ongoing efforts to reinvent dramatic language and contexts, as well as his awareness of the modern dramatic tradition and his individual talents.

THE AUDIENCE

Albee subverts the authority of his own dramatic text by casting the seers (the audience) into what is being seen (the performance). He delights in engaging the audience as concretely as possible. In *Who's Afraid of Virginia Woolf?*, he also places much responsibility on the audience. The playwright firmly believes that the ideal audience approaches a play without preconceptions or distorting labels, and with a capacity to suspend disbelief while immersing itself in the three-dimensional essence of the stage experience. He rejects the audience as voyeur. He courts the audience as active participants. Earlier we discussed Artaud's influence on Albee, and Artaud's theories perhaps become most discernible in Albee when we consider their relationship to the audience.

Albee's frequent reference in interviews to the French actor, director, and aesthetician Antonin Artaud is important. In 1938 Artaud, founder of the Theater of Cruelty, published *The Theatre and Its Double*, which quickly became one of the most provocative studies concerning the art of drama. Artaud tackles many issues in the book, including the civic function of the theater, and the way in which the theater can exteriorize metaphysical concerns. The dramatic experience should "disturb the senses' repose," should "unleash the repressed unconscious," and should precipitate nothing short of "a virtual revolt."[2] Cruelty, for Artaud, is the key alchemical ingredient that could generate an apocalyptic revolt within the audience—an audience Artaud viewed as the bourgeois Parisian who expected realistic performances. However, it is important to recognize that his theories extolling aggression and violence are grounded more in the cerebral and metaphysical than in merely the physical. His aesthetic imagination focuses on religious, metaphysical experiences that emanate from what he sees as the magical quality of live performance.

Albee, of course, does not stage the kind of theater Artaud envisioned: he would seem too conventional, too conservative, too reliant on language (despite his distrust of language in the later plays) for Artaud. But Artaud's influence is unmistakable in terms of Albee's use of violence on the stage. Referring to Artaud's influence on his own work, Albee emphasizes the value of staging militant performances:

> All drama goes for blood in one way or another. Some drama, which contains itself behind the invisible fourth wall, does it by giving the audience the illusion that it is the spectator. This isn't always true: if the drama succeeds the audience is *bloodied*, but in a different way. And sometimes the act of aggression is direct or indirect, but it is always an

act of aggression. And this is why I try very hard to involve the audience. As I've mentioned to you before, I want the audience to participate in the dramatic experience.[3]

Albee's theatrical strategy ideally minimizes the actor/audience barrier. As active participants in the play, Albee believes, the audience contributes to the ritualized forms of confrontation and expiation that characterize so much of his theater. This is why he sees Artaudian violence and death as finally and paradoxically life-giving:

> If one approaches the theater in a state of innocence, sober, without preconceptions, and willing to participate; if they are willing to have the status quo assaulted; if they are willing to understand that the theater is a live and dangerous experience—and therefore a *life-giving force*—then perhaps they are approaching the theater in an ideal state and that's the audience I wish I were writing for.[4]

LANGUAGE

Albee spectacularizes his stage first and foremost through language. As mentioned in the chapter on critical reception, he pays careful attention to the rhythms of his words and how they create, at times, a certain timbre. There is, at other decorous moments, an incantatory cadence to his prose. His verbal duels, some of which seem analogous to musical arias, are now a well-known part of American dramatic history. In both text and performance, Albee's technical virtuosity emanates from an ability to capture the values, personal politics, and often limited perceptions of his characters through language. "The accusative dialogue, and its cruelties" in *Who's Afraid of Virginia Woolf?*, contends Ruby Cohn, "are the wittiest ever heard on the American stage."[5] Similarly, C. W. E. Bigsby characterizes Albee's language as "By turns witty and abrasive, and with a control over language, its rhythms and nuances, unmatched in the American theater, he broke new ground with each play, refusing to repeat his early Broadway success."[6] His sarcasm and wit may also produce a comic language as well. True, the language from 1966 onward becomes more stylized, elliptical, even opaque; Albee's repartee—when he is at his best—still generates a compelling energy within each play. One of the chief tenets of *The Living Theatre*, writes Julian Beck, was to "revivify language," and through language the playwright might realize the civic and religious powers in the art of drama: *"to increase conscious awareness, to stress the sacredness of life, to break down the walls."*[7] Although Albee was in no way associated with the Living Theatre, the language of *Who's Afraid of Virginia Woolf?* captures the kinetic energy that Judith Malina and Beck felt so necessary for the stage. Albee's language valorized him.

PUBLIC ISSUES, PRIVATE TENSIONS

Who's Afraid of Virginia Woolf? spectacularizes Albee's lover's quarrel with American history and American thought. It is a quarrel that manifests itself through rebellious anger, but beyond its rebelliousness lies Albee's paradigm for the social contract, a model crystallizing the civic and personal confrontations informing all of his plays. Albee, it seemed, was the new Angry Young Man, a decidedly sociopolitical writer who anticipated, and then quickly became a spokesperson for, the social eruptions in the United States during the 1960s. Such plays as *The Zoo Story, The American Dream, The Sandbox,* and *The Death of Bessie Smith* cemented his reputation as a political writer, one whose rage existed in equipoise with his moral seriousness. *Who's Afraid of Virginia Woolf?* only strengthened the impression that, above all, Albee was a social protester blasting away at societal injustice and personal betrayal.

Although it is clear that Albee's early plays burgeon with sociopolitical textures, it is also equally clear that the real subjects of his plays preceding *Who's Afraid of Virginia Woolf?* have less to do with analyses of bigotry and a horrifying gulf between the haves and the have-nots than with explorations of internal forces—psychological, sexual, ethical, spiritual—that negate the possibility of the individual coming to consciousness. *The Death of Bessie Smith,* for example, pinpoints not so much a broader social malaise as a private individual failure of will that entraps its characters.

Despite experiments with dramatic language and structure, and the political overtones embodied in the plays, Albee invites us as we enter the hurly-burly world of *Who's Afraid of Virginia Woolf?* to attend to a kind of intuitive existentialist apprehension of George and Martha's experience. When Albee was a teenager reading the works of Albert Camus, he probably read the philosopher's suggestion in *The Rebel* that "The subject matter of art has been extended from psychology to the human condition." The human condition becomes the nerve center of *Who's Afraid of Virginia Woolf?*, an unmistakable moral dimension of Albee's vision. Throughout his career, in plays, college lectures, and private conversations, Albee alludes to the influence the existentialist movement exerts on his artistic vision. In an early interview, for example, he discusses the impact of the existentialist movement on the literary artist:

> The Existentialist and Post-Existentialist revaluation of the nature of reality and what everything is about in man's position to it came shortly after the 2nd World War. I don't think that it is an accident that it gained importance in writers' minds that it had now as a result of the bomb at Hiroshima. We developed the possibility of destroying ourselves totally and completely in a second. The ideals, the totems, the panaceas don't work much anymore and the whole concept of absurdity is a great deal less absurd now than it was before about 1945. (*CEA,* 36)

Such a "revaluation of the nature of reality," particularly within an existentialist context, has since become the unifying principle within Albee's aesthetic, and this principle informs the entire production of *Who's Afraid of Virginia Woolf?*. More recently Albee has reaffirmed the existentialist texture of this theater, highlighting what for him stands as the most compelling subject, consciousness. "The single journey through consciousness should be participated in as fully as possible by the individual, no matter how dangerous or cruel or terror-filled that experience may be. We only go through it once . . . and so we must do it fully conscious." Then Albee makes an observation that outlines his belief in the power of art to redeem. "One of the things art does is to not let people sleep their way through their lives," a point only too fully realized by George and Martha. "As all of my plays suggest," Albee adds, "so many people prefer to go through their lives semiconscious and they end up in a terrible panic because they've wasted so much. But being as self-aware, as awake, as open to various experience will produce a better society and a more intelligent self-government."[8]

The volcanic confluence of public issues and private tensions present in *Who's Afraid of Virginia Woolf?* is wedded to Albee's sense of consciousness. The preeminence of consciousness necessarily generates in George and Martha, and Nick and Honey, primal anxieties, dissociation, imbalances. If his heroes radiate gracelessness under pressure, Albee still maintains faith in the regenerative powers of the human imagination. This is the problem explored in *Who's Afraid of Virginia Woolf?*. Animating George's exorcism ritual is a recoverable awareness, a consciousness of his and Martha's pathetic condition.

Physical, psychosexual, and spiritual forces: these stand as the elements that so often converge within Albee's characters. This intermixture, moreover, precipitates an elemental anxiety, what Albee calls "a personal, private yowl" that "has something to do with the anguish of us all" (*AD*, 54). Accordingly, the power of *Who's Afraid of Virginia Woolf?* emanates not so much from any philosophical content as from its sheer artistry, which dramatizes humankind's struggle with the complex business of living. If George and Martha, with Nick and Honey, are to "burst the spirit's sleep," as Saul Bellow writes throughout *Henderson the Rain King,* such epiphanic moments are not easily grasped through the process of abstract philosophic intellection; rather, as Bellow's Gene Henderson discovers, these moments become comprehensible through the process of a concrete immersion in a cosmos that seems exciting yet hostile, reliable yet mutable, life-giving yet death-saturated. One of the thrilling dimensions of *Who's Afraid of Virginia Woolf?* concerns what ultimately becomes George and Martha's battle with precisely such a puckish cosmos that threatens them at every moment.

Albee's experiments with dramatic form at times place him within a postmodernist movement, but considering his dramatic oeuvre, the playwright harkens back to the Romantic tradition. Like Saul Bellow or Arthur Miller or Tennessee Williams, Albee believes in the talismanic powers of the aesthetic imagination and art to liberate, to create a liberal humanism. Underneath his characters' public bravado lies an ongoing inner drama, a subtext presenting the characters' quest for awareness. The tragic irony stems from the characters' inability to understand the regenerative power of consciousness. Nick and Honey appear to neglect the force of awareness—until George and Martha force them to reassess their own lives honestly.

For Albee, the play becomes the hour of consciousness. During this fleeting-but-illuminating hour, Albee's affirmative vision underscores the importance of confronting one's self and the other, without O'Neillean "pipe-dreams," or illusions. Further, his vision recognizes the benefit of regenerating the individual's spirit. Albee, in short, believes in the value and dignity of man. In the midst of a dehumanizing society, Albee's heroes, perhaps irrationally, affirm living. If O'Neill's, Ionesco's, or Beckett's characters seem aware of suffering, they also accept an attitude that precludes any significant growth. In contrast, Albee's heroes suffer, and dwell in an absurd world, but realize the opportunity for growth and change. Albee's heroes often experience a coming to consciousness that draws them, to allude again to that important metaphor in *Who's Afraid of Virginia Woolf?*, toward "the marrow"—that is, toward the essence, the core of their relationships. Stripped of illusions, Albee's protagonists stand naked. And once naked, they begin rekindling those forces that may profoundly alter their stance towards human encounters. Of course, Albee offers no guarantee of order, comprehension, survival, or love. Whether each character takes advantage of powers of consciousness remains unresolved at the end of *Who's Afraid of Virginia Woolf?*. On the other hand, Albee implies that, indeed, George and Martha, with their guests, will be shocked into awareness as Peter was at the end of *The Zoo Story*. Regardless of what may or may not be, an important point remains fixed: Albee's theater consistently stages the *possibility* that his heroes, and perhaps the audience, through the process of seeing and being seen, can become more honest with both their inner and outer worlds.

Thus, to regard Albee's use of verbal dueling and death as proof of a pessimistic vision is to overlook the haunting incandescence of *Who's Afraid of Virginia Woolf?*. Throughout his career, Albee has defined in dramatic terms, to use his own words, "how we lie to ourselves and to each other, how we try to live without the cleansing consciousness of death" (*TP*, 10). To experience the "cleansing" effects of such self-awareness, each player of his masterwork will be asked to question the nature of his or her values, predicaments, and relationships. To live honestly—as Jerry in *The Zoo Story*, and Grandma in *The Sandbox*, and Tobias in *A Delicate Balance*, and the Wife in *All Over*, and Charlie in *Seascape*, and Jo in *The Lady from Dubuque*, and Jack and Gillian in *Marriage Play* discover—frees the mind, even at the risk of facing a grimly deterministic world in which one suddenly feels the utter precariousness of existence. That certain characters fail to take advantage of this capacity to bear a world so conceived does not negate the significance of such self-perception, as Albee suggests throughout *Who's Afraid of Virginia Woolf?*.

8

THE CHARACTERS
Martha

In text, Albee describes Martha as a *"large, boisterous woman, 52, look-ing somewhat younger,"* a role for which Uta Hagen seemed perfectly suited. As an *"ample, but not fleshy"* woman, Hagen's physical presence correlated to the playwright's conception of his heroine. That physical impression was made even more famous when Elizabeth Taylor starred in the 1966 film version, and was reaffirmed when Colleen Dewhurst starred in the successful 1976 Broadway revival. Martha's physicality and outspokenness still invite the viewers or readers to perceive her as a self-destroying woman whose tirades earn her a reputation for being the overbearing, domineering, devouring female, a fully developed Mommy-figure from Albee's earlier work from Off Broadway. Indeed, Martha at first seems a reinvented and decidedly more terrifying Mommy-figure from *The Sandbox* and *The American Dream*, plays in which Albee takes great care in portraying his female leads as castrating manipulators of emasculated male figures. Particularly in *The American Dream*, the unsparing satire is directed toward the American family and what Albee views as a lamentable schism fueled by a loss of love, which separates one family member from the other and, on a social level, sepa-rates an entire nation from its own people. From a biographical viewpoint, perhaps Albee's own childhood accounts for part of that play's felt militancy. Financially, the Albee family was obviously secure: the young playwright was adopted into a multimillionaire household and "had private tutors and could command a reasonable array of servants."[1] Albee apparently viewed his mother as a domineering, even uncaring figure (physically, she was nearly a foot taller than her husband; psychologically, she seems to have developed a hostile attitude toward her family). According to the limited sources available concerning the playwright's childhood (even today Albee's past personal life remains off limits in interviews), his mother was the wife who tormented her weak, emasculated husband. The parents' wealth allowed them, it also seems, to substitute material pleasure for love. Perhaps these factors account for the anger of the early plays. Rejection, abandonment, loss of love, misplaced values, misspent energies, and withdrawals from human commitment dominate *The Zoo Story, The Death of Bessie Smith,* and *The American Dream.* Perhaps Albee's homosexuality only added to the strained relations between unloving parents and a child growing up in the 1940s and 1950s, and, in the plays, expresses itself through the tremendous animosity between the sexes.

Thus, Martha appears on one level as an extension of Albee's irreverent, hostile female figures, perhaps drawn from subconscious impressions and actual encounters with his mother and other females. Undoubtedly she is angry, frustrated, one who gains energy when venting her fury on anyone within her orbit. She may accurately describe George as "a drowning man [who] takes down those nearest" (223), but we also must concede that she participates in his "drowning" and seems incapable, or unwilling, to rescue him. Albee wastes no time in establishing her brashness; her litany of verbal taunts begins only minutes into the action, culminating in her explosive "SCREW YOU!"—an outburst of course meant for her husband but unceremoniously received by a stunned Nick and Honey, who are "*framed in the entrance*" (19). Indeed, throughout the play we hear little to dispel impressions of Martha as hostile, even evil. For example, George often refers to his wife in less than flattering terms: she is a "goddamn destructive" woman (46); George recalls an old photograph of Martha dancing with a man in a marathon dance contest, her "biceps all bulging, holding up her partner" (126). George at one point even implies that she may have sexually molested their son. She would break into his bedroom, her "hands all over his . . . " (120). He also calls her a "sub-human monster" (19). Later he refers to his wife in atheistic and demonic terms, which only adds to our ambivalent impression of Martha: she presides as "the only true pagan on the eastern seaboard" (73); a "SATANIC BITCH" (137); and a "Cyclops" (99). Hence our image of a vicious, demonic, even perverse Martha.

On another level, however, Martha emerges not so much as a wicked, domineering character, but as a profoundly troubled—and loving—woman. "I think she's a real gutsy three dimensional well rounded woman who can play the monster when she's thrust into that role," Albee explained in 1967, an observation pointing to her capacity to play any game during the evening when pressed (*CEA*, 87). Her tirades plainly exceed the limits of expected social devoir. Yet her psychology and interactions become more plausible (and understandable) when Albee provides subtle-but-telling glimpses into her past psychohistory. Like Jerry in *The Zoo Story*, Grandma in *The Sandbox*, and Julia in *A Delicate Balance*, Martha feels estranged, an interior detachment borne of parental loss and rejection. Minor details embedded in the script invite the observation. Her mother died when she was a child. Her father remarried an extremely wealthy "old lady with warts" (109) who never loved Martha, a point underscored when the stepmother's "big fat will" is handsomely divided between institutions (the township of New Carthage, the college) and others (Martha's father). Martha received "just this much" (110), a token sum indicating not the financial status, but the spiritual bankruptcy of the family. After the death of her stepmother, her father raised her and she in turn "absolutely worshipped" him (77). However, her father gradually detached himself emotionally from his daughter and, as she matured into womanhood, he only distanced himself further. Apparently, Albee implies, whatever she did to gain fatherly recognition fell tragically short of its purpose. He even arranged for the dissolution of her first marriage. "I was revirginized," Martha puts it (78), suggesting that he not only disapproves of her personal, private decisions, but indeed rejects everything that Martha is.

The Characters

The dissolved marriage is nothing less than the father's very public and symbolic projection of utter displeasure with Martha's entire *being*. Worse, Martha never leaves New Carthage, where her father is president of the college at which George teaches history, thus creating a geographical as well as emotional sense of entrapment. Although father and daughter maintain an outward show of family unity, as when they attend the same social functions at the college, George confirms the intensity of their estrangement by reporting that she lives in the shadow of a parent who "doesn't give a damn whether she lives or dies, who couldn't care less *what* happens to his only daughter" (225).

Martha's dismal relationship with her father has been forged by a lifetime of abandonment. Her feelings of being deserted by such an influential figure in her life explain her constant need to be heard. Her insistent prattling, her impulse to be the loci of all conversation, masks her sense of familial incompleteness and becomes a distraction as comforting as it is destructive. Ever fearful of abandonment, she thus always seeks engagement: with George, Nick, or Honey; with the gardener; with a father whose central interest concerns maintaining disinterest; with anyone who can violate her aloneness.

Albee spotlights her condition at the very start of act 3. Talking to herself in a form of private monologue, she suddenly says, "THE POKER NIGHT" (186). This is a reference, of course, to the original title of what would become Tennessee Williams's *A Streetcar Named Desire,* whose tragic heroine, Blanche Dubois, shares certain psychological affinities with Martha. Like Blanche, Martha has experienced and continues to fear rejection and abandonment, and thus quells her dread with alcohol, in the fabrication of illusions. And like Blanche, Martha cannot admit absence, aloneness, abandonment. Moments into act 3, Martha's internal reflections reveal a rare show of her actual feelings about her father: "Deserted! Abandon-ed!" And seconds later: "Daddy? Daddy? Martha is abandon-ed." And finally: "I cry all the time too, Daddy. I cry allll the time; but deep inside, so no one can see me" (185).

Albee further emphasizes the lack of love between father and daughter by denying him a proper name. Throughout the Albee canon, in fact, we may locate plays in which nameless characters appear: in such early plays as *Fam and Yam, The Death of Bessie Smith, The Sandbox*, and *The American Dream;* in such plays from the middle of his career as *Quotations from Chairman Mao Tse-Tung* and *All Over;* and in the more recent works—*Counting the Ways, Listening*, and *The Man Who Had Three Arms*. The lack of proper names is important to Albee, his method for minimizing the characters' humanity, for pinpointing the ascendancy of functional labels over human identities. The namelessness also correlates to the characters' spiritual deadness, for these are individuals whose egos so infiltrate their daily discourse that such humane values as love and compassion fade, become distant social forces. Thus by ascribing to Martha's father merely a functional title, Albee diminishes the father's humanity and intimates his inability to love his only daughter. Further, his professional station—president of a small, private, liberal arts college in New England—might (or should) imply that behind the title lies a humane person, and behind the person a caring, loving father. We are given no such evidence, however. Rather, he remains a defleshed functional type, a disembodied nonpresence: at best, the President of the College, Father, "Daddy," and at worst, a "white mouse" with "tiny red eyes" (109), but never a flesh-and-blood human being who responds to Martha.

The restorative power of love, which Jerry tried to understand in *The Zoo Story*, vanishes in the father-daughter relationship of this play. Love never becomes a force connecting Martha and her father. Most discernible by its absence, love collapses under the pressure caused by the father's blatant marginalization of Martha. Only hatred and indifference, Albee suggests, now inhabit the vacant spaces. In a sense, Martha comes to see her father much the way Virginia Woolf, the novelist, regarded Sir Leslie Stephen, her father. Woolf's father seemed sociable to the outside world, just as Martha's father undoubtedly appeared at the college functions. But to Woolf herself, Sir Leslie Stephen, like Martha's father, remained sufficiently detached. "When Nessa and I inherited the rule of the house," Woolf reflects in her *Moments of Being: Unpublished Autobiographical Writings*, "I knew nothing of the sociable father, and the writer father was much more exacting and pressing than he is now that I only find him in books; and it was the tyrant father—the exacting, the vi-

olent, the histrionic, the demonstrative, the self-centered, the self pity-
ing, the deaf, the appealing, the alternately loved and hated father—that
dominated me then."[2] Martha feels the range of emotions Virginia Woolf
felt toward her parent.

Hampered by her past psychohistory, Martha presently overcom-
pensates, it seems, by undercutting those with whom she can make contact. Thus she lashes out at one central male figure in her life, George,
and appears as the badgering, manipulative female, the controller and
castrator of a defenseless and emasculated husband. Only the other central male figure with whom she has a (fictionalized loving) relationship,
her son, can deflect her pain.

Psychologically forsaken, she tries to reinvent a loving home
through her marriage to a "bright-eyed" (81) George, who at the time
counterbalanced a sense of unrealized dreams by fulfilling her romantic
desires. "And along came George. That's right. *Who* was young . . .
intelligent . . . and . . . bushy-tailed, and . . . sort of cute" (81). However,
reality subverts her romantic heroic ideal during the course of a two-
decade-long marriage, her warring nature prompted by years of dulled
ambitions and diminished hopes.

Martha intuitively feels a sense of aloneness in the midst of company, dread in the everyday world, terror in the mundane. Whereas so
many other Albee figures face similar anxieties by retreating into anesthetizing, death-in-life social patterns, Martha fights back, refuses to surrender her will, her essential self. And this is precisely why Martha,
despite her self-destructiveness, gains a degree of heroic stature.

Albee works carefully to stage the existential authenticity of
Martha's flawed outer and inner world. Despite her energy, she radiates a
sense of world-weariness and, because such weariness seems hard to pinpoint, Albee presents her overall present condition as vague yet felt,
vague because her irreverence shrouds uneasiness, felt because she is
frightened about her very being in the world. William Barrett, in his well-
known *What Is Existentialism?*, discusses Martin Heidegger's *Angst*,
which correlates precisely with Martha's overall condition and Albee's
overall thematic concerns in the play:

Anxiety *(Angst)* is the fundamental feeling precisely because it is directed toward the world more plainly than any other feeling. Anxiety is indefinite: it is not about this or that object, we are simply anxious and we do not know about what; and when it is over, we have to say that "it was about nothing." This is what the psychoanalysts call free-floating anxiety; anxiety without any discoverable object. . . . What we are anxious about in such states, Heidegger tells us, is our very Being-in-the-world as such. That is why anxiety is more fundamental to human existence than fear. Fear is always definite; about this or that object in the world; but anxiety is directed toward our Being-in-the-world itself, with which every definite object, or thing, within the world is involved. Thus anxiety, more than any other feeling, discovers to us the world: i.e., brings us face to face with a world, to which we now sense ourselves to be in precarious relation.[3]

The forms of uneasiness and precariousness Barrett locates exactly correspond to Albee's portrait of his heroine. "In ordinary life," Barrett also suggests, "we usually evade the condition: we try to transform this indefinite anxiety into a definite fear or worry about this or that particular object. Thus authentic anxiety disappears, in our banal existence. . . . a state in which man perpetually busies himself with diversions and distractions from himself and his own existence. . . . "[4] Barrett describes the banality of those, as T. S. Eliot writes in *Four Quartets*, "Distracted from distraction by distraction." And because her *Angst* is so fundamental to her own existence, Martha desperately counterbalances her anxieties and unfulfillment through various distractions—drinking, parties, verbal dueling, Nick, and always George. Uta Hagen, in *Respect for Acting*, recounts how she had to draw on many personal relationships to exteriorize Martha's contradictory stances. "As Martha," Hagen writes, "in order to create the love-hate to George . . . I had to isolate *moments* of many relationships in which challenge, vengeance, wounding and vulnerability were at stake."[5]

The son-myth stands as Martha's greatest distraction. In his *Paris Review* interview, Albee says that both George and Martha recognize that their son is an illusion, but occasionally become "confused, when the awful loss and lack that made the creation of the symbol essential becomes overwhelming—like when they're drunk, for example. Or when they're terribly tired." Albee also points out that his lead characters are quite aware of the persistence of their illusion and that the son-myth represents "the most serious game in the world. And the nonexistent son is a symbol and a weapon they use in every one of their arguments" (*CEA*, 59). However, as the action unfolds, it becomes equally clear that Martha's identification with her fictional son is so real that she has lost sight of truth and illusion distinctions. Nick and Honey disturb her psychic well-being by acknowledging the presence of the son-myth, which in turn forces George and Martha to concretize the source of their uneasiness about their being-in-the-world. But as the myth dissolves during this particular evening, as necessary fictions give way to terrifying realities, Martha's psychological buffers can no longer sustain comforting illusions. Distraction cannot mask her emptiness precisely because her boundaries of sanity are disturbed by an acute awareness of her utter precariousness of being-in-the-world. "Anxiety," writes Barrett, "thus gives us the first clue to an authentic existence possible for the human person."[6] Within context of Barrett's ideas, Martha's histrionics and monologues of cruelty reveal both the authenticity as well as the destructive nature of her world.

In *Respect for Acting*, Uta Hagen reveals sections of her private workbook containing notes to herself regarding how she wanted to act out Martha's part. As the following excerpt indicates, the names that Hagen jotted down "belong to my personal life and suggest possible substitutions" for the lead characters in the play; items in brackets are Hagen's. What follows stands as much more than a fascinating chronicle of acting methods Hagen brought to each rehearsal. Her notes also reflect the divided loyalties and conflicting questions that plague Martha:

Late *Saturday* night. Late? As a matter of fact, 2 A.M. End of September = crackly red and yellow and brown leaves! *Frosty* night? Hot indoors? Edward means it all to be now. [1962.] The new college term just opened. Booze! Football practice? Did I go this afternoon? Who's the coach? = Bradley. Yummy. New semester = faculty teas, heavy drinking at cocktail parties = tension, hysteria from new students, new faculty = the Johnstons, the Garricks, etc.

The party at Daddy's house tonight. A dozen new faculty members. Particularize them! Especially meeting with Nick and Honey = Marian and Dave? Or Marian and Bill? *How* did I show off? - how much to provoke George? Or to impress Daddy? I sang, "Who's Afraid of Virginia Woolf?" I'll bet I read *Orlando* last week! [A novel by V. Woolf] I "brayed." *When?* What about? Boxing? History? Status? We never discuss politics. Were George and I stung?—Remember McCarthy! [And I don't mean Eugene!] Am I aware of new political movements among young faculty members—like Nick? Or students? Do I try to participate with them? Uh-uh. Cynical, skeptical intellectuals—both George and me. Atheists. Agnostics? = Max and Alicia.

George in the History Department = Art History = Papa's assistants = power plays, like in corporations = also faculty wives jockeying for position = Jack S., maybe Ruth—Oh, yes, yes, yes.

The house is *messy.* Pretentiously unpretentious living! Ugh. Scatter rugs = Prof. Alex's house = Books piled sideways on shelves. Disorder, and = *unwatered* plants. Maybe an instrument lying open? Or the record player? Yes! Hahaha. Open and ready to go. Loose records lying around. The *Eroica?* Or the *Missa Solemnis?* Worn upholstery on "good" furniture. I think it's an *old* house—properly antiqued and comfy. Mortgaged? Is it a "home"? Nope. *Make* the neighborhood = mix together Adams St., Lathrop St., and Walton. *Make* the campus specific = mix up Ithaca, Madison, and Bennington = Faust [Prof. Albert Faust, my uncle].

This town is New Carthage. What was *old* Carthage? I remember some Roman, like Caesar, said, "Carthage must be destroyed!" Edward's symbols? How apt!! Too intellectual for me—can't use it!!! I was born and raised in New Carthage = Wisc. High, maybe Randall school. Grew up in Daddy's—college pres. mansion = Phil R's house. Did I brag about the mansion? Did I feel lonely there? Did I like somebody else's "home" better? = Jane Mc. Where am I vulnerable to Daddy? When I was little? Now? Vulnerable to George? What areas? Not just *age.*

Make the street = elms, maples, burnt-orange mums—eeek! Neighbors = the W's, they weren't faculty, more conventional. When we come home, George says. "Sssshhh, the neighbors!" Can they hear us making a racket even when we're in the house? During the play?

Make the rest of the house. Have to work on the *bedroom!* The kitchen!—with Nick. The bathroom with Honey! Where do I usually park in the living room? My favorite chair? Are there toys around for our "child"????? Daddy's portrait or photo? Ask Edward if I can use one of Papa. Wow![7]

Hagen's notes to herself clearly reflect the Martha Albee wishes to project: a noble, valiant woman plagued with self-contradictions, self-doubt, and blessed with an iron will.

Martha is the architect of her own predicament. Victimized by her losses, she apparently does little to better herself. "Without any sense of how she can contribute to improve the quality of her life," Anita Maria Stenz explains, "expecting all things great and beautiful to come from outside herself, she wallows in disillusionment. With nothing to do that interests her and nothing to live for, she spends her nights leaving a trail of half-filled glasses of gin around the house and her days sleeping off her drunkenness."[8] As such, Martha becomes a prisoner confined within her own self-erected house of games. Feeling more rejected than loved while growing up, she squares her disappointments on challenging and sometimes rejecting others—especially George. She knows that she is victimized by her own contradictory impulses. Thus Martha feels imprisoned in a suffocating familial trinity: first by her father, then by her husband, and finally by her very self.

GEORGE

Ostensibly George appears in control. He endures public insult and private innuendo with valiant composure, particularly when Martha changes the rules of the games without warning. Rational, self-restrained, George delicately balances the drama, and his equanimity plays counterpoint to Martha's capriciousness. An urbanely gracious man concerned with the closing of the American mind, George appeals to the audience's rational faculties, his capacity to maintain ballast a welcome response to the maniacal occurrences unfolding on the stage. One critic goes as far as to see George as the "tragic anti-hero," one who is "highly intelligent and sensitive, an idealist trapped into a marriage with a demanding wife and controlled by" her father.[9] While it is true that he has his (anti)heroic attributes, it seems equally true that we risk oversimplifying Albee's portrait of George if we view him solely as a noble hero struggling against insurmountable odds, an anti-hero whose evenmindedness somehow saves him socially, whose belief in humanistic principles elevates him morally.

For George is also accountable for the current status of their fictional and actual world. He contributes to their troubled welfare in several ways, but none more telling than in the abdication of his own spirit. By choice, he has experienced a gradual shift in human intercourse, a shift from engagement to habit, from commitment to estrangement. George's seemingly noble efforts to preserve marital and psychic order ironically promote his and Martha's spiritual inertia, the ossification of their entire relationship. Even his verbal inventiveness, honed over the years as a survival measure, may be seen as a way of gaining an upper hand with others. His language, at times, is as manipulative as it is communicative. His words may torpedo as much as rescue their relationship. To be sure, he must rely on verbal dexterity for his and Martha's well-being, but sometimes his language ambushes the other: language often turns into a conscious weapon to sabotage, control, or subjugate those around him. He obviously has personal qualities and an intellectual curiosity that make him markedly different from the emasculated Daddy figures of *The Sandbox* and *The American Dream*. George is a fully developed character whose insights qualitatively separate him from the other male figures within Albee's theater. Still, in certain respects his social strategy over the years has evolved into a corrosive force almost as devastating as the public and private withdrawals of other pivotal male figures in the Albee canon: Peter in *The Zoo Story;* Julian in *Tiny Alice;* Tobias in *A Delicate Balance;* the Son in *All Over;* or Charlie in *Seascape.* George has drifted away from the "total engagement" that the Mistress in *All Over* knows must exist within a relationship (*AO,* 14). Professionally as well as personally, George has compromised his being, retreating to his books as a safeguard, as a convenient and outwardly acceptable way of avoiding confrontation.

Whereas other important male figures in Albee's theater often appear as stock character types—the reticent publishing executive, or the retired suburban businessman, for instance—George is complex, a portraiture of soaring human desires mixed with plummeting human faults. Albee is at his best when capturing the dialectic nature of George's personality. George's strength of will is neutralized by his weakness of heart. He can endure insult and yet, at times, he deserves Martha's wrath. He is at once the embodiment of stability and great good sense as well as an image of impotency and mediocrity.

One scene especially hints at George's inadequacies. Martha recounts how, years ago, on impulse she suddenly pummeled her husband with a "roundhouse right" that, in the presence of her father and guests, sent George sprawling into the bushes (56). Her story plainly embarrasses George. As she finishes, George quietly appears with a short-barreled shotgun, "*calmly aims it at the back of Martha's head*" (57), and pulls the trigger. This is one of the most suspenseful moments in the play, for Albee again blurs traditional distinctions between realism and fantasy: for just a few seconds, the audience believes that it is about to witness the murder of Martha. "You're dead! Pow! You're dead!" (57). George triggers the Hemingwayesque shotgun, which suddenly blossoms into a parasol—and a richly symbolic display of George's power and weakness. On the one hand, this is triumphant game-playing, George's clever way of asserting his potency over the others, his means of scoring yet another point in the games they play. (In the film version, the scene becomes one of the most riveting encounters in the action: the camera eye telescopes in on a possessed George stalking his prey; a building drum beat embellishes an emotionally charged confrontation, and we are led to think that this scene surely will culminate in cold-blooded murder.) Even Martha concedes that her adversary has played the game with great panache. Everyone blinked. On the other hand, despite George's theatricalism, the audience is equally struck by the parasol as the symbolic equivalent of sexual impotency. The scene, after all, comes after Martha has just scored a point in their games by challenging George's manliness, by questioning his masculinity. Her recounting of the past when her father insisted that he and George box; and how George shyly declined; and how she leveled him with one punch; all these details recreated in the presence of Honey and a former amateur boxing champion, Nick: surely this story reveals, or so George thinks, a true lack in his maleness. Further, Martha's feigned sexual interest in Nick—"You don't need any props, do you, baby?" (61)—only calls additional attention to George's alleged sexual paralysis. Although George clearly denies all suggestions to the contrary, Martha further threatens her husband's pride: she even implies that "deep down in the private-most pit of his gut, he's not completely sure it's his own kid" (71). Questions about George's ability to maintain order in his own house arise when Martha screams, "I wear the pants in this house because somebody's got to" (157). In any event, the Chinese parasol, in all its *"large red and yellow"* colors (57), becomes the negative phallic symbol. Any possible erotic connotations regarding its sexual virility as symbolized by the shotgun instantly become rendered flaccid after its climax—a mere parasol as George's only sign of sexual (im)potency.

George and Martha, then, become what Shakespeare calls mighty opposites: they thrive off the destructive give and take that so ennobles and so enervates their relationship. They are, in Albee's words, "equal competitors."[10] "There is some secret understanding between them," explains Paolucci. "She has ruined him with her excessive demands and her domineering ways; but he has not been crushed."[11] This is precisely the kind of dialectic, infused with conflicting emotions and motives, that so characterizes their shell-shocked relationship.

Thus in a sense George invites Martha's vengeance. As the unacknowledged legislator of their inner world, George has proven less than satisfactory. He was, Martha explains, "expected to *be* somebody, not just some nobody, some bookworm, somebody who's so damn . . . contemplative, he can't make anything out of himself, somebody without the *guts* to make anybody proud of him . . . " (85). George's social strategy of withdrawal, Albee suggests, expands into a nearly death-in-life pattern, his intellectual screens blocking him from attending to the self and the other with any genuine energy or purpose. Early in the play

The Characters

Martha calls him a "PHRASEMAKER!" (14), a pointed reference, not merely to his skills with words but to his use of words as a form of concealing, or hiding behind, the truth. Nick, for one, feels the lexical pressure George can exert: "I'll play the charades like you've got 'em set up. . . . I'll play in your language. . . . I'll be what you say I am" (150). And minutes later Martha seconds the point, venting the frustration that comes when dealing with one whose language often seems more opaque than illuminating: "Have you ever listened to your sentences, George? Have you ever listened to the way you talk? You're so frigging . . . convoluted . . . that's what you are. You talk like you were writing one of your stupid papers" (155–56). Later, in the midst of one of Martha's heated tirades and flirtation with Nick, George calmly sits down to read a book—at 4:00 A.M. In part, of course, George deliberately plays games with Martha: in the heat of battle, when she expects, indeed, desires confrontation—"you pay attention to me!" (173)—he matches her fevered antics with inaction. He marginalizes Martha's outbursts by entering into his intellectual house of games, calmly reading a book while she carries on. The actionlessness of his action frustrates Martha, who thrives on the overt theatrics of her gamesmanship. Thus, on one level he scores a point in the game they are playing.

Considered from another angle, however, George's absorption in mental activities is reminiscent of Peter in *The Zoo Story*. Jerry chastises Peter for escaping from his wife, children, and certainly Jerry himself by reading, by what in context emerges as an intentional retreat from this stage of siege, from painful human encounters; it is a conscious relinquishing of the individual's impulse to take responsibility for his actions. Anesthetizing routines too often preempt honest engagement. Albee emphatically establishes the point in the play when George admits:

> I'm numbed enough . . . and I don't mean by liquor, though maybe that's been part of the process—a gradual, over-the-years going to sleep of the brain cells—I'm numbed enough, now, to be able to take you when we're alone. I don't listen to you . . . or when I *do* listen to you, I sift everything, I bring everything down to reflex response, so I don't really *hear* you, which is the only way to manage it. (155)

George has fallen prey to routine habits, what Samuel Beckett in *Waiting for Godot* calls "the great deadener" within human experience. Beckett influenced tremendously Albee's emerging aesthetic, as Albee himself points out, and we can easily trace his three-decade preoccupation with the Beckettian theme of spiritual inertia and cultural entropy, ideas which have long been hallmarks of Albee's dramaturgy. George's admission of feeling "numbed," then, outlines one of the play's central themes and underscores what has engaged the playwright's moral imagination for years: the necessary impulse to transcend any public or private decision that vitiates *being* itself. In *Who's Afraid of Virginia Woolf?*, only George seems to realize this distinction; moreover, only through George will the others, by the final curtain, begin to come to consciousness.

THE BERGIN STORY

Albee provides the audience with incomplete references to George's past. Details remain vague. But what seems clear is that, like Martha, George has been traumatized during his youth. Although Albee embeds details throughout the text, one of the most revealing accounts of George's past occurs in act 2—Walpurgisnacht, the traditional old German witches' Sabbath. Such a title for the act, with all its mysterious and ominous connotations, signals an intensification of the games the characters will play. It further signals the start of a deeper, more damaging unwinding process in which the characters expose more of their own inner realities. For example, Albee raises questions concerning one of George's adolescent rites of passage, earning a driver's license, and the way in which the pastness of this particular event affects his present condition. I refer to the Bergin story, the tale in which George's preparatory school acquaintance, while learning to drive, swerved to miss an animal, demolishing the automobile against a tree and killing his father. These events in and of themselves, although tragic, are unremarkable; but the psychic aftershocks the boy experienced inexorably changed his world, for his entire existence essentially ended after he learned of his father's death. Albee is well-known for his use of a story-within-a-play technique, one

The Characters

he employs successfully in *The Zoo Story* with Jerry's "Dog Story;" in *Tiny Alice* with Julian's bizarre story of a sexual encounter, which he may or may not have consummated, with a woman who claimed to be the Virgin Mary; and in *A Delicate Balance* with Tobias's "Cat Story." The Bergin story of *Who's Afraid of Virginia Woolf?*, though brief, is another example of Albee's use of such a narrative technique, one adding to the audience's growing sense of uncertainty about George's past. George wraps up the unsettling Bergin story for Nick:

> He was not killed, of course. And in the hospital, when he was conscious and out of danger, and when they told him that his father *was* dead, he began to laugh, I have been told, and his laughter grew and he would not stop, and it was not until after they jammed a needle in his arm, not until after that, until his consciousness slipped away from him, that his laughter subsided . . . stopped. And when he was recovered from his injuries enough so that he could be moved without damage should he struggle, he was put in an asylum. That was thirty years ago.

> *Nick:*   Is he . . . still there?
>
> *George:*   Oh, yes. And I'm told that for these thirty years he has . . . not . . . uttered . . . one . . . sound. (96)

The boy's hysteria and subsequent retreat into madness objectify the negative epiphany, an incomplete and distorted reenactment of Oedipal myths whereby the boy has succeeded horribly in (accidentally?) murdering his mother with a shotgun months before (accidentally?) murdering his father with the car. Albee keeps additional details shrouded in mystery, forcing the audience to draw conclusions more from implication and imagistic association than from logical deduction. Devoid of logical connectives, the Bergin story functions as a mystery tale whose full plot is left unresolved, whose characters remain in soft focus, whose very incompleteness and messy inconclusiveness only add to the building ominousness of the entire play, where fictional or real violence and destruction hover just behind a thin layer of realism and threaten to explode at any given moment. In *Who's Afraid of Virginia Woolf?*, Albee never lets the audience rest.

The Bergin story gains its theatrical and thematic power through the accretion of symbolic and psychological connections with George's past, and as such suggests other disturbing parallels. For beyond the events and muted violence directed toward the parent figure in the Bergin story lie more immediate possibilities: perhaps George is the substitute speaker for the boy in the story.

More specifically, the audience never knows exactly if, indeed, the boy is merely a persona for George and if the nonfiction novel to which his father-in-law so vociferously objects is George's way of coming to terms with his own appalling past, a form of expiation. Ambiguous and mysterious, the story-within-a-play complements the broader truth/ illusion motif of the drama. This is where Albee consciously undermines the authority of his own script. He delights in keeping the audience off balance, for we never know if George is a "stage magician" or not: is he giving us, as Williams poeticizes in *The Glass Menagerie*, an "illusion that has the appearance of truth" or a "truth in the pleasant disguise of illu- sion"? The ambiguity and mystery of the Bergin story increase with Martha's never-fully-explained remarks: she claims "something funny" in George's past haunts him to this day and that, once the truth reveals it- self, he will have wished he "died in that automobile" (154). According to Martha, George's past directly corresponds to the Bergin story. His past mimics the horrifying events of the past tale and are reinvented in his unpublished nonfiction novel. If the audience believes Martha, and the evidence supports her claims, the boy in the Bergin story is nothing less than George's persona. In other words, George killed *his* father exactly the same way the boy did and, by implication, killed *his* mother the way the fictive boy did. Albee strengthens the correspondence between George's fictive and actual experiences by elevating emotional intensity, the verbal duel turning, for the first time during the evening, to the physi- cal assault:

> *Martha:* Georgie said [to Martha's father] . . . but Daddy . . . I mean . . .
> ha, ha, ha, ha . . . but *Sir,* it isn't a *novel* at all . . . (*Other voice*)

> Not a novel? (*Mimicking George's voice*) No, Sir . . . it isn't a novel at all. . . .
>
> George: (*Advancing on her*) You will not say this!
>
> Nick: (*Sensing the danger*) Hey.
>
> Martha: The hell I won't. Keep away from me, you bastard! (*Backs off a little . . . uses George's voice again*) No, Sir, this isn't a novel at all . . . this is the truth . . . this really happened . . . TO ME!
>
> George: (*On her*) I'LL KILL YOU! (*Grabs her by the throat. They struggle*)
>
> Nick: HEY! (*Comes between them*)
>
> Honey: (*Wildly*) VIOLENCE! VIOLENCE! (*George, Martha, and Nick struggle . . . yells, etc.*)
>
> Martha: IT HAPPENED! TO ME! TO ME!
>
> George: YOU SATANIC BITCH!
>
> Nick: STOP THAT! STOP THAT!
>
> Honey: VIOLENCE! VIOLENCE! (*The other three struggle. George's hands are on Martha's throat. Nick grabs him, tears him from Martha, throws him on the floor. George, on the floor; Nick over him; Martha to one side, her hand on her throat*)
>
> Nick: That's enough now! (136–38)

Martha's cruel remarks undoubtedly are her way of retaliating against George, the events of the Bergin story exaggerated, perhaps, to humiliate. Yet she introduces a more disconcerting and decidedly more tragic scenario. She also implies that George did not merely cause his parents' accidental deaths but deliberately murdered them. Deriving pleasure from George's discomfort, Martha pushes on: "Imagine such a thing! A book about a boy who murders his mother and kills his father, and pretends it's all an accident!" (136). Moments later she chants, "Mur . . . der . . . er" (138). George, himself, lends credence to her charges when his own version of the story is, in Anne Paolucci's words, "strangely similar to the account in the original story."[12] The scene occurs as he brings the exorcism to its climax:

> George: Martha . . . (*Long pause*) . . . our son is . . . dead. (*Silence*) He was . . . killed . . . late in the afternoon. . . . (*Silence*) (*A tiny*

chuckle) on a country road, with his learner's permit in his
pocket, he swerved to avoid a porcupine, and drove straight into
a. . . .

Martha: (*Rigid fury*) YOU . . . CAN'T . . . DO . . . THAT!

George: . . . large tree. (231)

The reader or viewer can never amass enough evidence to decide posi-
tively if George's nonfiction novel concerns the Truth—the allegedly actual past tragedies of his own life. However, George's violent reaction to
Martha's accusations add to the mysterious undercurrents running
throughout the play and may explain why he presently withdraws from
human engagements, preferring the solitude of reading and thinking
more about abstract concepts—history, the decline of Western civilization, eugenics—than such concrete realities as his relationship with his
parents, Martha, his own inner condition, and what can be done to repair
the ruins of his past. Further, just the idea of George as creator of and
participant in his novel's nonfictional events suggests that he is as vulnerable, anguished, and confused as Martha. Except for a few outbursts in
which he verbally or physically attacks Martha, he is simply more capable
of masking his flawed inner condition. Like Martha, he has immersed
himself within fantasy. Their individual fantasy worlds dovetail, of
course, with the child-illusion.

In the final analysis, however, George must be seen as exerting a life-
giving, preserving influence in the play. Whereas many other Albee heroes succumb to a grimly deterministic universe, George is presented as
transcending his own considerable limitations to redeem his and
Martha's lives. There is no other figure in all of Albee's theater who can
match George's dramatic and ethical stature; in fact, in many respects he
stands as one of the more compelling figures in all of modern American
drama. He is intelligent and clever, shrewd and thoughtful, the only one
in the play with a heightened sensibility. An historian, he is entranced by
the contiguities of cultural attitudes and the moral imperatives forged by
preceding civilizations. George, alone, takes a moral stand against scientific determinism, against conformity, against reason shorn of passion.
He does not challenge Nick the man as much as the principle upon

which Nick has founded his professional values, and the tyrant whose monomania established such principles in the first place. Above all, George historicizes Albee's masterwork. Through the sweep and play of evolutionary and historical patterns, George implies, humankind has the unique capacity to transcend noble savagery and the purely animalistic response to human nature, to become separate, thinking beings whose mentor is reason. For Yank in O'Neill's *The Hairy Ape* or Stanley in Williams's *A Streetcar Named Desire*, such quality of thought seems beyond their ken, and they ultimately seem imprisoned within a Darwinian naturalistic cosmos. For Willy in Miller's *Death of a Salesman*, the gap between instinct and reason narrows, but Willy, too, seems engulfed by a malevolent universe and emerges as a naturalistic victim as well. The Tyrones of O'Neill's *Long Day's Journey into Night* feel the pressure exacted by the naturalistic universe. George is different. Of tremendous importance to George is the necessary balance of reason and passion, the rational faculties leavened with emotional capabilities. The dominance of a purely rational stance toward the self and the other, George argues, poses a distinct threat to the human species. It is a qualitative stance. For George, the private experience of the individual defines the public issues of a nation and, finally, of human existence itself. Ever engaged with the personal and the public function of history and its relationship to science, George continually reflects on (Martha would say he gets bogged down by) the puckish roles of fate, humane values, science-as-truth, definitions of the social contract, and their influence on what Arthur Schlesinger would call the "cycles" of American history and thought.

George possesses a compelling integrity, a belief in certain humanistic moral principles. Although he has not distinguished himself as an historian and withdraws into his own self, George earns the audience's sympathy and admiration— sympathy because of an ability to withstand the emotional hazing, admiration because of an ability to restore a qualitative order, based on love, to his marriage by the final curtain. One of his most significant insights is understanding that *both* he and Martha have "moved bag and baggage" (155) into a psychotic make-believe world; that *both* suffer from a collective inability to accept truth over illusion; and that their games have descended into a form of madness. But the chief difference between the two concerns objectivity: he alone detaches himself from the illusion, and is thereby able to help Martha restore psychic equilibrium. Undoubtedly, the play may be regarded as a battle of the sexes. *Who's Afraid of Virgina Woolf?*, despite its contemporaneity, harkens back to other classics in the modern tradition imbued with gender conflicts: there are intimations of George Bernard Shaw's *Heartbreak House,* Henrik Ibsen's *Hedda Gabler,* and August Strindberg's *The Dance of Death,* plays whose reputations lie largely in their sophistication of language and subtlety of psychological exploration of sexual tensions. And yet to dismiss (as many scholars have) Martha as the castrating female and George as the emasculated house boy oversimplifies their psychologies and the existentialist quality of their relationship.

As there is always a sense of violence lingering just below the façade of social composure, so too is there the one central force that ultimately triumphs: the love George and Martha share. Each knows about the other's inadequacies, and each knows that the other will be able to rise above the spiritual bankruptcy that, left unchecked, threatens to destroy their world. Albee confirms the point when, at the beginning of act 3, Martha acknowledges her authentic love for her soul mate:

> . . . George who is out somewhere there in the dark. . . . George who is good to me, and whom I revile; who understands me, and whom I push off; who can make me laugh, and I choke it back in my throat; who can hold me, at night, so that it's warm, and whom I will bite so there's blood; who keeps learning the games we play as quickly as I can change the rules; who can make me happy and I do not wish to be happy, and yes I do wish to be happy. George and Martha: sad, sad, sad. (190–91)

Armed with such an ability to absorb changes in the rules of the game, George sets his sights on banishing the greatest failure and most debilitating illusion from their existence.

The Characters

NICK

Nick is a caricature. The newly appointed assistant professor of biology seems to represent an innocent midwesterner. The theatergoer initially sympathizes with the young man: he appears too polite to refuse Martha's invitation to the after-party party at her home, too aware of departmental politics to offend those in lofty places (George and Martha, after all, are fixtures at the college), and too obedient to extract himself and Honey from what instantly escalates into a socially awkward endurance test. Most in the audience have some sympathetic correspondence with a person who tells George, "I just don't see why you feel you have to subject *other* people" to ridicule (91). Albee stresses the social uneasiness of Nick and Honey, particularly at the moment of their entrance, and the audience feels for the naive, well-meaning couple that is ambushed and unwittingly trapped in the emotional cross fire.

Nick is no match for his guests. From the moment he makes his awkward appearance, George tests the intelligent, youthful scientist one moment, derides him the next, ever shifting any comfortable field of social reference so that Nick can never be sure if he is interpreting signals accurately. Near the beginning of the action, for instance, Nick recognizes that his host will involve him in social game-playing and will verbally spar with the younger amateur boxer:

> All right . . . what do you want me to say? Do you want me to say it's funny, so you can contradict me and say it's sad? or do you want me to say it's sad so you can turn around and say no, it's funny. You can play that damn little game any way you want to, you know! (33)

In spite of Nick's protest and impulse to leave—he remarks that he prefers never to "become involved" in the "affairs" of business associates (34)—George refuses to let him escape. George delights in keeping Nick off-balance, ever beguiling, cajoling him into lowering his public guard and surprising the thirty-year-old when, in a gesture of *"comforting a child,"* he declares that becoming involved in business associates' affairs is the norm at the college: "Musical beds is the faculty sport around here"

(34). Lured, no doubt, by continual drink, George goads Nick, who takes his clues from George and goes along with the games while simultaneously playing into George's hand, because he is never sure of the exact rules. Although he is clearly the object of manipulation, Nick only gives George more reason to attack when confessing that his professional ambition marginalizes human concerns. This is a Nick who will, on a professional level, (plot to) take over courses from his older colleagues in the biology department, will "start some special groups" for himself, and above all will "plow a few pertinent wives . . ." (112). Of course, Nick in one sense merely plays along with his adversary; he is a reluctant participant in drunken banter—it is his supposedly innocuous way of enduring a very long business obligation. But Albee's theatrical strategy depends on (or encourages) the collapse of traditional truth and illusion distinctions, as seen when Nick raises the ante in the game, suggesting that he will seduce Martha. "Well now, I'd just better get her off in a corner and mount her like a goddamn dog, eh?" (114). The exchange turns more threatening after George entices, then implicates, his rival:

> George: Why, you'd certainly better.
>
> Nick: (*Looks at George a minute, his expression a little sick*) You know, I almost think you're serious.
>
> George: (*Toasting him*) No, baby . . . *you* almost think you're serious, and it scares the hell out of you. (114)

Nick's eagerness to rise in the profession through sexual proclivity soon deflates itself for, when put to the test, he fails in one of the games, "Hump the Hostess." Martha's flirtation with Nick is simply her way of escalating her war with her husband. Nick is reduced to an impotent boy. Martha chides him, George humiliates him. "Look! I know the game! You don't make it in the sack, you're a houseboy" (202).

The audience's impressions of Nick as innocent midwesterner changes to Nick as opportunistic scientist. In many ways, he stands as the latest version of the Albeean American Dream figure. In *The American Dream*, The Young Man defines an absurdist type, an exaggerated spineless caricature who is the target of Albee's satire. The Young Man, like

The Characters

Nick, is "almost insultingly good looking in a typical American way. Good profile, straight nose, honest eyes, wonderful smile" (*AD*, 107). More importantly, behind the attractive façade, Albee implies, lies a defleshed functional type, a vain incarnation of a sterile culture, one who readily admits that he, as consummate conformist, will "do almost anything for money" (*AD*, 109). As another kind of conformist, "a pragmatic extension of the big dream" (145), Nick also will do almost anything to rise in professional rank, including sabotaging anyone blocking his efforts to succeed. The Young Man of the earlier play appears drained of all substance and individuality, one of the few figures in the Albee canon who can be regarded as a truly absurdist character. Nick, on the other hand, becomes more than a blatantly dislocated stock American Dream figure; worse, he has evolved into a more sophisticated, intelligent, elaborately detailed, indeed, a more sinister extension of The Young Man. Significantly enough, only Nick lacks, not just a past family history and personal biography, but some traumatic event that has forever altered his being. (The only details Albee provides are that Nick and Honey's families have been lifelong acquaintances, he earned a master's at nineteen, and he was a good boxer.) Denied a past, Nick squares his synthetic hopes on a future that will be solely determined by distilled scientific truths forged from an amoral and sterile present. Within Albee's scenario, Nick lacks the moral gravity of George, and such moral inadequacy, for George, must not go unchallenged this particular evening.

Nick represents what Henry Hackamore in Sam Shepard's *Seduced* symbolizes—the "nightmare of the nation." For Albee as for George, Nick stands for a new generation of scientists who subordinate human ideals to a pragmatic view of life. Such an attitude certainly permeates Nick's personal life, as evident when he reveals that family pressure and social decorum, not love, motivated him to marry Honey. "I wouldn't say there was any . . . particular *passion* between us, even at the beginning . . . of our marriage, I mean" (105). Like Peter's marriage in *The Zoo Story* or Tobias's in *A Delicate Balance*, Nick's marital relationship seems physically as well as spiritually inert. His stance toward Honey devalues any heroic romantic ideals; replacing passion and love are biology and finances. Nick admits that Honey's father, a corrupt evangelical, left his daughter financially secure, which undoubtedly attracted Nick to her even more. Nick and Honey are Albee's clearest symbols of public and private sterility, and complement his larger thematic concern in the play. *Who's Afraid of Virginia Woolf?* is Albee's grand lament for a loss of love, a loss of humane values, a loss of the self and the other. Nick's directing force in life centers on professional and monetary, not familial, satisfaction; and Honey, by not resisting, only ratifies their American Dream pursuits. Nick will be successful, Albee implies, because of the young scientist's a priori belief in the myth of the American Dream and a society that prizes the pragmatism of these "wave-of-the future boys" (107). His innocence long ago corrupted, as ideals gave way to expedient compromises, Nick places his faith and love in an entrepreneurial America and has become almost machinelike: he possesses "steely-blue" eyes, a "solid gold groin" (111). Nick represents a new and disturbing kind of professoriate of which George wants no part and against which he rebels. "I will fight you, young man . . . one hand on my scrotum, to be sure . . . but with my free hand I will battle you to the death" (68). Appalled by everything Nick stands for, George admits that he feels threatened on a private level (Nick may seduce his wife) and on a public level (he may undermine the Jeffersonian principles so dear to George).

Feelings of threat and subversion partially account for George's deliberate melding of boundaries separating truth and illusion. Indeed, George shifts alliances with Nick constantly. He creates the impression, in Nick's mind at least, that there exists some kind of male bonding between them and that, as faculty of a small liberal arts college, they somehow share certain educational principles—hence their ostensible collegiality and drunken banter about their wives and how they came into some inheritance. In fact, quite the opposite is the case, as George, while suddenly shifting some unstated alliance with Nick, admits:

> You realize, of course, that I've been drawing you out on this stuff, not because I'm interested in your terrible lifehood, but only because you represent a direct and pertinent threat to my lifehood, and I want to get the goods on you. (111)

The Characters

Such potential threats, Albee suggests, emerge from much more than the possibility of Nick seducing Martha. Albee's real interest lies with charting broader social mythologies. The lessons of history, and how they have been conveniently ignored, lie at the heart of Albee's masterwork. Nick, the potential shaper of future history, faces George, the torchbearer for past history. George takes it upon himself, as a Thoreauvian surveyor of human history, to assume a liberal humanistic stance toward the outer world.

Nick, a seemingly indeterminate figure, plays an integral role in the playwright's ideographic presentation: his single-minded, scientistic vision of experience, and all the dehumanizing cultural connotations which Albee would like the audience to ascribe to Nick, elevate him to the status of a decadent, even evil, major character. Nick acts as a foil to George and all the ideals on which George bases his life. Nick and George create a marvelous dialectic within the play, dramatizing as they do Albee's exploration of the connections between the individual's sense of public responsibility and his or her definition of private liberties. This is essentially a Tocquevillian dialectic that, on the one hand, recognizes the individual's right to pursue vigorously professional and entrepreneurial interests. Nick fills this role within the paradigm. On the other hand, this Tocquevillian dialectic also posits that in an ideal world, such private interests should, but do not, exist in equipoise with a purposeful sense of civic and moral duty. George, of course, represents this part of the paradigm. Albee's dialectic and its underlying tensions produce in Nick and George divided alliances and contribute to the play's multivalency and ambivalent intensity.

Albee seems drawn toward certain civic issues with which Alexis de Tocqueville grappled in *Democracy*, his seminal examination of American culture and thought. The heart of Tocqueville's beliefs, explains historian Arthur Schlesinger, centers on the ambiguous (and probably irreconcilable) interconnections of public ideals and private interests: "The great distinction, in short, between the classical republics and modern democracy lay in the commercial motive. . . . The problem was to make private interest the moral equivalent of public virtue. This could be achieved through the disciplinary influence exerted by society on its members—an influence embodied in the mores and in law and institutions. *Self-interest rightly understood:* this Tocqueville saw as the key to the balance between virtue and interest in commercial values."[13] The delicate moral balance between the public and the private which so engaged Tocqueville exerts an equally strong influence on Albee's aesthetics in general, and his conceptualization of George and Nick in particular. In Albee's scheme, George is the standard-bearer of noble public virtue, Nick of smug self-serving enterprise and self-aggrandizement.

In *The Sandbox* and *The American Dream,* Albee anticipated all that Nick symbolizes through an investigation of the same ideological and mythic terrain forming the crucible from which rises the American Dream myth. Such a cultural milieu invites an ironic treatment of experience and, in *Who's Afraid of Virginia Woolf?*, Nick and Honey become the primary agents producing, and absorbing, such ironic satire. Echoing his prefatory remarks to *The American Dream,* Albee alludes to the historiography of *Who's Afraid of Virginia Woolf?* by naming George and Martha as he did. In 1965 Albee remarks that "there was some notion in my mind, while I was working on the play . . . which is the reason actually that I named the couple George and Martha—after General and Mrs. Washington. There might be an allegory to be drawn, and have the fantasy child the revolutionary principle of this country that we haven't lived up to yet."[14] Later Albee again makes the analogy: "Indeed," Albee said in 1966, "I did name the two lead characters of *Virginia Woolf* George and Martha because there is contained in the play . . . an attempt to examine the success or failure of American revolutionary principles" (*CEA,* 58). And two decades after the debut of the play, he remarked that *Who's Afraid of Virginia Woolf?* was "the result of my examination of the 50s, as much as anything. Many of us suspected that even though we were terribly enthusiastic about the Thousand Days of Kennedy before terribly long it would be business as usual and things could slide back to the way they were. And, indeed, quickly enough they did" (*CEA,* 162). Through Nick, Albee objectifies not merely a post-Eisenhower belief in science as truth (a notion made more urgent when Albee conceded that he named Nick after Nikita Khruschev), but a lament for a decline of values in Western civilization. Through Nick, Albee reinvents in dramatic terms what Tocqueville observed in historical terms a century before: that private self-interest, unchecked by moral conscience, inevitably leads to self-collapse. In summing up Tocqueville's theories, Schlesinger writes: "Self-interest wrongly understood tilts the balance away from republican virtue and from public purpose. The individual withdraws from the public sphere, becomes isolated, weak, docile, powerless. Individualism in the Tocquevillian sense leads to apathy, apathy to despotism, despotism to stagnation, stagnation to extinction. The light dwindles by degrees and expires of itself."[15] Albee places Nick in just such a dismal pattern. In *Who's Afraid of Virginia Woolf?*, informed social or public responsibility threatens to turn into anomie. Only through the paradoxical nature of George and Martha's cleansing influence will Nick and Honey be able to break out of this destabilizing pattern. For Albee, as for Tocqueville before him, self-interest rightly understood is "the key to the balance between virtue and interest in commercial democracies."[16] Within Albee's presentation, George understands this vital distinction. Nick does not.

HONEY

In performance, the actress playing Honey provides a much-needed source of comedy. Her lines and body gestures allow for some hamming, which eases the tension of the stage action. In text, Honey becomes the most cartoonish figure in the play, a woman "who blushes over any mention of sex and has about as much substance as cotton candy."[17] Whereas the others calculate their next move while criticizing the others' motives, Honey skims along the surface unfazed by the verbal skirmishes erupting around her. In fact, she assists George and Martha's performance by asking the inane or predictable question, by interjecting the innocuous or clichéd response at the perfect moment, thereby making George and Martha's responses appear even more vituperative and clever. Moreover, Honey accepts her husband's patronizing and falsely solicitous gestures, and appears least equipped to deal with the evening's strangeness. This becomes especially noticeable when she encourages George to proceed with his "Get the Guests" story, even though she is initially unaware that the story concerns her private affairs. Her very stage presence—her body movements, pleasant manners, banal assertions—suggests that she has no ax to grind and certainly is not weighed down by some larger philosophical quarrel with the nominal world. Like Nora at the start of Ibsen's *A Doll's House,* Honey prides herself on acting chipper and sparkly, always placing her husband's professional needs and personal desires before her own wishes. Like Nora (before her cataclysmic epiphany at the end of Ibsen's play), Honey appears subjugated by her husband and willingly trivializes herself: she, too, is a doll-like figure whose every word and deed seem controlled by invisible strings, a puppet within her own contemporary version of a doll's house. Albee's stage directions throughout delineate Honey as a comedic doll whose submissiveness matches her airheadedness.

Grandma in *The American Dream,* Miss Alice in *Tiny Alice,* Agnes in *A Delicate Balance,* The Mistress in *All Over,* Nancy in *Seascape,* Jo in *The Lady from Dubuque*—these female characters from other Albee dramas, in spite of their personal betrayals and tragedies, are intelligent, feisty, shrewd, dominant, sometimes bitchy, strong, and capable of independent intellectual and emotional judgments equaling or far exceeding their male counterparts. Honey surely is the most humorous of all Albee female characters, but she ranks near the bottom in terms of gutsiness and quality of thought. She is the pliable, submissive "wifelet" (205). Polite and quick to observe propriety, she attends to social appearances. With Nick, she completes their image as the young, bourgeois middle-class couple who, through hard work and unwavering devotion, will rise to become living symbols of the American Dream. Looks triumph over substance.

However, Honey possesses more substance than most scholars acknowledge. Beneath her undeniable comedic façade lies a tremendous amount of anger and frustration and, beyond that, dread and terror. She is, like Williams's Maggie, a cat on a hot tin roof, a woman plagued by anxieties only hinted at by a skittishness that masks her deeper unfulfillment. And her feelings of unfulfillment neutralize her impulse to analyze her marital inadequacies. Like Peter in *The Zoo Story,* she prefers not to learn anything about unpleasant realities or unpredictable contingencies. Desiring love and companionship, she ironically never enters into a meaningful relationship with Nick. The result, to use Jerry's words from *The Zoo Story*, translates into nothingness: "What is gained is loss" (*ZS*, 36). Her role as a kind of Shakespearean fool functions as a social buffer, neatly preventing involvement in vital human intercourse. Like Martha, Honey's past emotionally paralyzes her present world. And such emotional stasis, despite her well-meaning intentions, promotes the spiritual bankruptcy that so characterizes her marriage. Maintaining a delicate balance in *Who's Afraid of Virginia Woolf?*, for Honey, means sustaining an entropic present. Her assumptions and attitudes neatly preserve what T. S. Eliot in *Four Quartets* calls "the mental emptiness" paralyzing her world. Honey perceives the incompletions and disassociations of her life and marriage, but elects to maintain the comfortable holding pattern that preserves her ossified spirit.

Albee joins the comic with the tragic in portraying Honey's death-in-life existence. Isolated, alone, and, until act 3, invulnerable, Honey assumes a thematically central role in the play's psychodynamics. More so than any other character, she represents the tragic breakdown in the pragmatics of human discourse. Her language and funny gestures tend to gloss over the splits between words, meanings, and deeds, splits that grow increasingly more noticeable as her life unwinds before the viewer or reader. Her language not only defines but confines her very place within the world. Her banal chatter entraps rather than explains.

Albee accentuates Nick and Honey's spiritual aridity by focusing on their psychological and biological barrenness. (It is fittingly ironic that Nick, the young, potent scientist, may be incapable of fathering children.) Further, their contributions to the play allow the audience to view Nick as more than an emotional punching bag and Honey as more than a comedic doll. In certain significant ways, the younger couple's relationship mirrors George and Martha's. The most conspicuous parallel concerns the childlessness of the two couples.

Who's Afraid of Virginia Woolf? is a ritual concerning two couples incapable of having children. George and Martha, pressed by their own inverted reasoning, must concede that their son has reached his majority. Accordingly, they must participate in the boy's rite of passage and involve themselves in a valediction: he must leave. Similarly, Nick and Honey, pressed by their own series of denials, must admit that their nonchild has not even been given a chance to reach birth, not to mention majority. Throughout her life, Honey has entered into an elaborate pattern of sub-terfuges, a set of public and private denials and repressions relative to her (and/or Nick's) inability to conceive a child. Thus she erects illusions as an O'Neillean anodyne. Throughout his life, Nick has broached conven-ient public rationalizations meant, not to deny his or Honey's infertility, but—simply and decidedly more tragically—to avoid the messy and complex business of living itself. Nick's problem may (or may not) be a matter of genetics. But clearly a source of impotency lingers elsewhere: in his unwillingness to communicate honestly, or what the existentialists would call authentically, with the self and the other. Not once does Nick ask Honey about their childlessness—or, really, about anything. Further, Albee implies that he has probably never engaged Honey as a human being capable of original insight and emotion; he has never tackled their sexual condition whose infertility in all likelihood is based more in psy-chological than biological breakdowns.

Nick and Honey's childlessness has its roots in the stillbirth of their relationship. Both were attracted, we are led to believe, to each other by surface appearances—what Willy Loman in *Death of a Salesman* calls "personal attractiveness"—rather than deeper, more honest primal con-nections. Theirs was a shotgun marriage, a hastily arranged ceremony in-spired by Honey's pregnancy. Like Martha's pregnancy, however, Honey's is but an illusion:

> Nick: She wasn't . . . really. It was a hysterical pregnancy. She blew up, and then she went down.
> George: And while she was up, you married her.
> Nick: And then she went down.
> (*They both laugh, and are a little surprised that they do*) (94)

Thus from its inception, Nick and Honey's marriage was based on de-ception and self-betrayal. Honey is not married to Nick; she is wedded to fear itself: fear of commitment; of bearing children; of authentic relationship; of living with heightened consciousness. The extent of their non-marriage becomes obvious after she learns of Nick's divulging their most private condition to an outsider. Nick's confession to George about the hysterical pregnancy violates their agreement to remain silent about his nonpresence and also parallels George and Martha's revelations of their son. Despite strong differences, the two couples thus share knowledge of intimate fantasies.

George lays bare the younger couple's repressed anxieties in his "Get the Guests" story. This is another important story-within-a-play because it introduces additional parallels between the players and their respective childless condition, and strangely parallels the Bergin story insofar as it reveals mysteries of the past while confirming the couples' overreliance on illusions as their only way of compensating for the barrenness of their present. These stories-within-the-play, then, reflect one of Albee's primary structural strategies in *Who's Afraid of Virginia Woolf?*: to dredge up uncomfortable crux moments from the couples' past—Martha's knockdown punch of George, George's unpublished novel, a father's rejection of his daughter, fathers who plunder churches and colleges for personal wealth, Honey's hysterical pregnancy, the supposed presence of George and Martha's son, for instance—and represent these painful or embarrassing encounters, not only because they give the playwright a chance to showcase his storytelling virtuosity, but because they imply just how far from objective reality his characters have strayed. It is a near-fatal distance. Thus the two couples share more than a child-illusion; they also share a sensibility that has allowed for its creation in the first place and a vulnerability that has insisted on its continuing presence. Further, both couples disclose a kind of spiritual hemorrhaging process that threatens their sanity, for both have descended into forms of madness: the stories-within-the-play, in which they are central protagonists, certify their tortured psychologies.

In the form of rituals, these past stories become parables, the contents of which are shaped by some traumatic experience that has hastened that character's present emotional paralysis. Honey, for example, fabricates her own story-within-a-play, although she is the listener of her own tale first told by Nick to George, then retold by George to all. Her false pregnancy hardly can be seen as her way of ensnaring a mate. But it clearly emerges as a diversionary stratagem by which she can avoid reality: her terror of having children. Nick only contributes to her self-imprisonment by discouraging her from talking about the truth. The inability to communicate her predicament to her husband has led to a marriage predicated mostly on social appearances, not love. Honey remains satisfied, even happy, as long as her prized illusions remain. And her strategy plays directly into Nick's role as the dominant (and domineering) partner within their one-sided (non)relationship. Further, Honey often acts and speaks as a child would, adding to the pathetic impression that she has not grown much past an embryonic stage.

Ironically, Nick and Honey's presence in their hosts' home functions exactly the way Harry and Edna's intrusion will in *A Delicate Balance*: they introduce Terror, disturb the psychic well-being of the hosts, and destroy George and Martha's complacency and private mythology, which have come to blot out reality. Edna's existentialist confession about the sheer emptiness of their lives—"WE WERE FRIGHTENED . . . AND THERE WAS NOTHING" (*DB*, 47)—mirrors Honey's similar revelation:

> NO! . . . I DON'T WANT ANY . . . I DON'T WANT THEM. . . . GO 'WAY. . . . *(Begins to cry)* I DON'T WANT . . . ANY . . . CHILDREN. . . . I . . . don't want . . . any . . . children. I'm afraid! I don't want to be hurt. . . . PLEASE! (176)

Her outburst testifies to the intensity of a deep-rooted anxiety with which, to this point, both she and Nick have not come to terms. By admitting to her existentialist fear, Honey paves the way for the hazardous possibility of an authentic life with the self and the other, a possibility that becomes more manifest when she finds the courage to announce near the play's end, "I want a child. I want a baby" (223). Her words have a cathartic influence, signaling a first step in facing reality shorn of illusions. No longer, Albee implies, will George be able to refer to Honey as "angel-tits" (129) or "a wifey little type who gargles brandy all the time" (142). Albee has said of Nick and Honey:

The Characters

There might have been some humanising going on during the course of the play to him [Nick]. I don't know the extent to which Nick and Honey will be able to go on with their lives. They may have to alter a bit themselves . . . in the play all that is suggested is that you clear away all the debris and then you decide what you are going to do. It doesn't say that everything will be all right at all. O'Neill suggested that you have false illusions in order to survive. The only optimistic act in *Who's Afraid of Virginia Woolf?* is to say, admit that there are false illusions and then live with them if you want and know that they are false. After all, it's an act of public exorcism.[18]

Honey, Albee further suggests, will also force Nick to rethink the nature of his life and marriage, just as George and Martha's honesty at the play's end forces them to reassess their lives. As such, Honey may be viewed as much more than a comedic doll, even though she would probably have preferred to remain under the influence of her illusions and the relative comfort afforded by her superficial posturing. With her epiphanic moment, however, her life with Nick has undergone the first stage of a profound reformation. Albee does not guarantee that Honey's sunburst of insight will forever improve her life, but he clearly suggests that her transformation, initiated within the chrysalis of George and Martha's home, is a distinct possibility.

9

THE SET AND SETTING:
FROM REALISM TO NONREALISM

When the theatergoer took his or her seat in the Billy Rose Theatre, he or she in all likelihood was quickly taken with the arrangements on the stage. Alan Schneider, the famous director of numerous Beckett plays, worked closely with William Ritman, the designer (both of whom worked on many later Albee productions before their deaths in 1984) to reproduce with exactitude Albee's intention. Today Albee acknowledges his indebtedness to Schneider, whom he had first met when the then-unknown playwright's *The Zoo Story* had its American premiere with Beckett's *Krapp's Last Tape,* which Schneider directed. "Alan was an extraordinary director," Albee told fellow playwright Terrence McNally in 1985. "He only directed plays he had some respect for. Since he did respect them, his interest was getting the author's intention, whatever it was, whether it was right or wrong. He would try to help the author a little bit here and there. Not to impose, but to get the author's intention onstage as accurately and as clearly as possible. . . . He was the kind of director who would want to have conversations six months before rehearsals began. He would keep coming with lists of twenty, thirty, forty questions to ask me about the play. . . . Alan was an intelligent and dedicated man" (*CEA,* 198–99). The collaborative design for the stage set was

The Set and Setting: From Realism to Nonrealism

instantly recognizable and comfortably "naturalistic" (in the theatrical sense of "realistic" as opposed to the influential Naturalistic period in literary history). As a set mirroring objective reality, there is something graspable about its overall arrangement. Its physical makeup is one that the audience can easily comprehend. The overall image of the set seems wedded to a truthful, objective representation of the real world, founded on the playwright's meticulous perceptions of contemporary manners and life. In essence, the rather ordinary set functions as a culturally coded sign as well as a simulacrum, or mirror image, of objective reality: this is a realistic play set in a realistic place and will unfold within a realistic time frame. Through its straightforward spatial realism, the set captures a sense of Aristotelian unity.

There is little resemblance to the expressionistic setting of Strindberg's *The Ghost Sonata* or such early O'Neill plays as *The Hairy Ape* or *The Emperor Jones*. Nor do we find in this Albee set the existentialist minimalism of Beckett's stage in *Happy Days,* the poetic lyricism implicit in the set of Williams's *The Glass Menagerie,* the nonrealistic set of Miller's *After the Fall,* or the exaggerated sets of the German playwright Georg Kaiser—especially in *From Morning to Midnight* and his important *Gas* trilogy. In these more avant-garde sets, the director, designer, and playwright emphasize highly stylized equivalencies for various subjective states of mind and being, rather than the realist's scrupulous fidelity to the actual particularities of how, say, a living room must appear. Often through the use of music, highly distorted or fragmentary exchanges, or an emphasis on the dreamlike or grotesque, the dramatist interested in nonrealism seeks to exploit the plastic quality of the performing arts: lights splashing across the stage to suggest a character's interior frame of mind, as seen in Elmer Rice's *The Adding Machine*. Often the playwright employs rhythmic music and percussion instruments to underscore a particularly tense moment, as evident in Strindberg's *A Dream Play* or *There Are Crimes and There Are Crimes*. The playwright's nonrealistic set sometimes achieves its power from what Brecht calls *Verfremdungseffekt,* a "strange-making effect" which elicits from the spectator feelings and imagistic associations of alienation, while keeping that spectator, as Martin Esslin puts it, "detached from the action, safe against the temptation of being sucked into it."[1] Other stage sets are meant to suggest the melding of time, as achieved in Miller's *Death of a Salesman,* where the audience witnesses the simultaneous presentation of three kinds of time—psychic, social, and chronological. Albee, of course, experiments with nonrealistic sets in *The Sandbox, The American Dream, Box,* and *Quotations from Chairman Mao Tse-tung.* But does he in his masterwork?

The set of *Who's Afraid of Virginia Woolf?,* by contrast, seems grounded in everyday, verifiable reality. The theatergoer sees an Ibsenesque, realistic stage: a couch and coffee table, the stuffed chairs, the bar, booze, and glasses, the rugs, lamps, portraits, and stacks of books in the wood-paneled book cases, all objects representative of the mimetic theory of art—a coherent and consistent formulation, a direct imitation of human places and possessions. Such stage props are a deliberate choice on the playwright's and director's part, for above all these props create an overriding impression of contemporaneity—this is a play situated in the here and now by an artist who is of his time. This is a play whose contemporaneous stage world embodies as closely as possible a direct one-to-one correspondence with the natural order of the world. The set implies that the audience will confront an unidealized world of George and Martha and, by extension, many of the customs and mores characteristic of life in the United States circa 1962. Art imitates life. In text, Albee provides little in terms of stage notes. He simply describes the scene as *"the living room of a small house on the campus of a small New England college."* Yet all of the subsequent fleeting references to the stage set reinforce its realism. In both text and performance, this is how, we are led to believe, a history professor and his wife living in a small New England town might live—the props convey an image of a comfortable, well-used home that probably reinforces certain subconscious "realistic" impressions and expectations in most members of the Broadway audience.

And yet, despite the overt realism of the set, Albee deliberately sabotages mere objective mimeticism. By melding the natural, verifiable world with a figurative, imaginative world, Albee's set contributes to a nonrealistic ambiance, atmosphere, or environment. Again, this is a subtle shift, not the blatant nonrealism of Sam Shepard's *Operation Side-winder* or Eugene Ionesco's *Amédée*. Albee never explicitly denotes through stage directions such a nonrealistic quality, but the Ibsenesque surface naturalism of George and Martha's home suggests something of a *claustrophobic* set. Many, including the playwright himself, have referred to the stage environment as an entrapping, almost suffocating stage world. The womb-like setting in this play does not necessarily nurture life-giving forces, but rather externalizes the characters' spiritual inertia. Albee's stage set, suggests Bigsby, "stands as an image of a refusal of life by those who enact their fears and illusions with it."[2] Thematically, the melding of an ostensibly realistic set with symbolic fields of reference—social, political, existential—contributes to Albee's theatrical intent: to present a stage world of seemingly comforting illusions that ultimately collapse of their own critical mass and implied inadequacies. The home of George and Martha, and all the events transpiring within its walls—the colloquial language (regarded as offensive during the play's initial Broadway run), the fairly conventional representation of plot, rising action, suspense, climax, resolution—all the dramaturgic elements of the play invite verisimilitude. But there is a subversive dynamic at work within Albee's set and its influence on the reader or viewer. The effect both bedevils and delights the audience. As Anne Paolucci observes, "the aberrations, the horrors, the mysteries are woven into the fabric of a perfectly normal setting so as to create the illusion of total realism, against which the abnormal and the shocking have even greater impact."[3] C. W. E. Bigsby further explains the impact of Albee's strategy: "The apparently reassuring nature of the naturalistic set for *Who's Afraid of Virginia Woolf?* is, indeed, itself a tactic for ambushing an audience whose expectations are thereafter systematically frustrated."[4] Coming to terms with the physical as well as symbolic dimensions of the set, as Paolucci and Bigsby imply, is central to an audience's understanding of Albee's complex theatrical stratagem. As the characters enact games both real and fictional within this set, so the set, itself, becomes a visual and imagistic device for underscoring the psychodynamic of the games through its own "ambushing" effect.

The subversive influence of the set was undoubtedly more keenly felt by the first Broadway spectators, who were accustomed to traditional, predictable, safe productions that would not threaten orthodox theatrical tastes. This is the difference between the Off Broadway aesthetic and the conservative expectations of the Great White Way. Writing plays long before Off Broadway, the innovative German dramatist Georg Kaiser essentially pinpointed this distinction and would undoubtedly call the standard Broadway production *Schauspiele,* or plays whose glitz limit them to mere "spectacles," as contrasted with *Denkspiele,* or "thought-plays" designed to challenge audiences through experimental structures and sets. *Who's Afraid of Virginia Woolf?* is, after all, the product of an Off Broadway dramatist who, by great good luck, succeeded in staging what at the time was seen as a nontraditional work before a fairly conservative audience. Albee, as much as anyone, was pleasantly astonished by the opportunity to challenge the conservatism of Broadway with his masterwork. Shortly after the play stormed Broadway, Albee recalled:

Who's Afraid of Virginia Woolf? was produced by the same two men that I worked with as producers all the way along the line of Off-Broadway, Richard Barr and Clinton Wilder. These were two men who had both produced on Broadway and they didn't like Broadway very much—they didn't like the compromise and the corruption of Broadway. And so they decided more or less simultaneously to produce Off-Broadway where plays are allowed to exist on their own terms. So we all got together by great fortune and we started working Off-Broadway and it was their intention to bring the Off-Broadway standards to Broadway. And for some reason which can be explained only by them, the first play they decided to do on Broadway was one of mine— *Who's Afraid of Virginia Woolf?* But what we did . . . was to decide just to do a play exactly as we would have done it Off-Broadway, which means that we got the best actors for it and we got the best director for the play . . . Barr and Wilder produced my play . . . for $42,000 which was unheard of, because most Broadway productions today [1963] cost upward of $100,000. The money bit is important because theater costs have been priced out of sense and intelligence, and this attrition leads to high ticket prices; it leads to the theory that a play must please all of the critics or close because it is so expensive. (*CEA,* 28–29)

The Set and Setting: From Realism to Nonrealism

Albee's setting, like the set itself, also subtly but importantly contributes to the play's complexity and multivalency. Albee locates his set in a house on the campus of a small liberal arts college. The college setting has its own rich symbolic overtones, not because of any particular geographical site, but because of its relatedness to art, politics, and morality, and the necessary freedoms that ideally are associated with the examination of various aesthetic, scientific, and philosophical disciplines. The college-as-setting becomes yet another element of Albee's theatrical conception, and becomes thematically central to the overall "ambushing" impact of the play. For the setting will ultimately underscore and thereby intensify the loss of love and human relationship that Albee seems intent on dramatizing. As Bigsby argues, "the university is conventionally regarded as the centre of a particular kind of freedom, as the embodiment of liberal humanist values, and hence betrayal here is the more profound and disturbing."[5]

Albee's set and setting even take on allegorical overtones after we learn the name of the township in which the action takes place—New Carthage. Carthage was the ancient city located on the northern shores of Africa, its name coming from the Latin *Carthago*, which was a derivative of the Phoenician name meaning "new city." Founded in the ninth century B.C., the city-state was "the scene of one of the greatest love stories in all history, that of Dido and Aeneas,"[6] a point of tremendous irony given the subject of Albee's play. Dido, according to one legend, threw herself on a flaming pyre to avoid marrying the King of Libya; in Virgil's *Aeneid*, she falls in love with Aeneas only to destroy herself after he, upon Jupiter's demand, leaves to continue his journey. In any event, the mythological richness of the Queen of Carthage's plight undoubtedly intrigued Albee, and its thematic resonance cannot be dismissed when examining *Who's Afraid of Virginia Woolf?*. The "newness" of the ancient city emerged mostly from its economic vitality, and by the sixth and fifth centuries B.C., thanks to the city's expanding network of trade and commerce, Carthaginians became a dominant force in the western Mediterranean. Perhaps because of what George deems "historical inevitability" (114), Carthage was doomed by a series of events—the Romans triumphed in the Punic Wars, culminating in the total destruction of

Carthaginian influence and power in the Third Punic War (149–46 B.C.), during which Roman soldiers razed the entire city. Preceding its demise at the hands of the Romans, however, internal dissension arose among Carthage's aristocracy of nobles and wealthy merchants. Essentially governed by a close-knit group of leading families and merchants, Carthage's political as well as moral structures began crumbling because of internecine warfare, or as George might say, "internal subversion" (125). Inspired by corruption and selfishness, the ruling class of Carthage was oligarchical in nature. Power and money cancelled out human compassion, it seems. Appropriately enough, there are few archaeological remains of ancient Carthage. Again, Albee uses the apocalyptic backdrop of Carthage's demise as an integral part of the historiography of his play.

George's passing references to the Punic Wars (94) thus only cohere what at first glance seem to be simply offhand, humorous asides. In another scene, he first equates his present home in New Carthage with Illyria, which immediately brings to mind the idealized fictional seacoast setting in Shakespeare's *Twelfth Night*. Albee's sardonic wit is at work here, however, for historically the Illyrians were prone to war and often engaged in piracy. Further, as with Carthage, the Romans conquered Illyria after several wars in 156 B.C., 119 B.C., and 78–77 B.C. The destruction implicit in Illyria's past will be reexperienced, on a domestic scale, in Albee's New Carthage, a point that only becomes more alarming when George suddenly interjects allusions to Penguin Island and Gomorrah:

> And this ... (*With a handsweep taking in not only the room, the house, but the whole countryside*) ... this is your heart's content— Illyria ... Penguin Island ... Gomorrah. ... You think you're going to be happy here in New Carthage, eh? (40)

Although never fully developed, his casual references to such infamous ancient cities and past events serve as George's way of reminding his guests about the lessons of history while, more significantly, adding to the allegorical and apocalyptic undercurrents of the entire play. The Penguin Island allusion, a reference to Anatole France's novel *Penguin Island,* complements the thematic design of the play insofar as it raises similar issues—for Anatole France, those issues were the satirization of French history; the relationship of truth and illusion; and the destruction of the island itself. For Albee, his play is (among many other things) a satire of contemporary American history; it concerns the interconnections between truth and illusion; and it dramatizes how deterioration of humane values, unless they are recovered and restored to their rightful place within the social contract, may lead to the (at least symbolic) destruction of the country itself. Similarly, the Gomorrah allusion also contributes to the play's thematic unity. Like Carthage and Penguin Island, Gomorrah was a city whose destruction was precipitated, in part, by its own vices. In the Bible, Gomorrah was destroyed along with Sodom by fire from Heaven, an act of divine retribution brought on by the city's carnal wickedness. It was the city, of course, where Lot's wife was transformed to a pillar of salt. Another layer of irony surfaces when we realize that Gomorrah was probably situated in the southern portion of, appropriately enough, the Dead Sea. The threat of an analogous kind of decadence and annihilation, Albee suggests throughout the play, may doom his heroes as well as our culture, if the Nicks of the world are left unchallenged and if the Georges of the world continue to withdraw from genuine human commitments.

The playwright's use of these historical-mythological-biblical references thus makes *Who's Afraid of Virginia Woolf?* more than a "realistic" drama emphasizing plot and character. The effect of Albee's use of such tantalizing allusions—the gradual accretion of symbols, the web of unfolding metaphors that reveal deeper meanings—invite the audience to see the play as a paradigm for the decline of Western civilization and any claims civilization may have on humane compassion. At least this is what Albee had in mind when, months before the play was staged, he said, "[*Who's Afraid of Virginia Woolf?*] has something to do with what I thought *The American Dream* had to do with—the substitution of artificial for real values in this society of ours" (*CEA*, 17). Taken in isolation, George's comments naturally may seem trite, even superficial—a cocktail party series of witticisms. Viewed in their full intertextuality, however, his remarks about Carthage, Gomorrah,

Penguin Island, Illyria, Berlin, and even Majorca, assume broader theatrical and social implications.

George claims to have once sailed past Majorca, the Balearic island off the Mediterranean coast of Spain. In and of itself, sailing by beautiful Majorca, which today thrives mainly on tourism, appears absolutely insignificant. Still, it too is interrelated with George's previous references to Carthage. Like Carthage, Majorca experienced a decline soon after Peter IV of Aragon took the kingdom from James II and restored it with the crown of Aragon, mostly because of changes in trade routes after the discovery of America, but also because of warfare between the local peasants and the Aragonese nobles and Catalan merchants. The historical events of Majorca are in no way as volcanic as those of Carthage, yet the subtle parallels only add to Albee's myth-making stratagem within the play. The Majorca allusion takes on additional resonance when we realize that the island, which has been inhabited since prehistoric times, was at one time occupied by Carthaginians and their conquerors, the Romans. Finally, George at one point labels Martha a "Cyclops" (99), an insult that has even broader suggestions when we discover that in Majorca there are many remains of a primitive technique of masonry construction of prehistoric times, a technique referred to today as "Cyclopean." Even the possible allusion to Homer's Cyclops works in context of Polyphemus' cave: the huge stones serving as the walls and entrance entrap Odysseus' crew, just as in symbolic terms Albee's set entraps his players. Perhaps these interconnections are easier to grasp in text than in performance, but collectively they form luminous patterns that strengthen the structure of the play and its imagistic textures. This technique has long been employed by dramatists, of course, and Esslin, in *An Anatomy of Drama,* points out the beauty of such methods:

> The total structure of a dramatic work thus depends on a very delicate balance of a multitude of elements, all of which must contribute to the total pattern and all of which are wholly interdependent. . . . Context is all: in the right context an almost imperceptible gesture may move mountains, the simplest phrase may turn into the most sublime poetic utterance. That is the true miracle of drama, its true poetry.[7]

The Set and Setting: From Realism to Nonrealism

The cumulative, dynamic structural interdependence that Esslin discusses captures the theatrical impact of George's references to history and myth. Such interdependence also accounts for the power of mimetic representation embodied within the play, a representative dimension that gives the work, in text or performance, its particular intensity.

10

To the Lighthouse: The Exorcism

> I have learned that neither kindness nor cruelty by themselves, inde-
> pendent of each other, creates any effect beyond themselves; and I
> have learned that the two combined, together, at the same time, are the
> teaching emotion.
>
> —Jerry in Albee's *The Zoo Story*

Act 3, "The Exorcism," is to Albee's play what the final section, "The
Lighthouse," is to Virginia Woolf's *To the Lighthouse*: the turning point
as well as an overall image of resolution and unity. The ending of Woolf's
novel, which occurs in September, the same month in which the play is
set, focuses on Lily's bringing the pastness of her past to her present
world, a brave new world that, despite death, reflects for Lily harmony, a
newfound wholeness. It is fitting that *To the Lighthouse* was, for Woolf,
an *exorcism*, a way for her to come to terms with the anxiety of influence
her parents exerted on her. Giving *To the Lighthouse* "emotional vividness, authenticity, and a genuine sense of intimacy," Alice van Buren
Kelley reminds us, "are the models behind the Ramsays, Virginia Woolf's
own parents, who walked like powerful ghosts through her life until she
exorcised them here."[1] It also seems fitting that Albee prepares both
Martha and the audience for the kind of questions on which Lily dwells
near the end of *To the Lighthouse*. "Was there no safety? No learning by
heart the ways of the world? No guide, no shelter, but all was miracle, and
leaping from the pinnacle of a tower into the air? Could it be, even for
elderly people, that this was life?—startling, unexpected, unknown?"[2]
These are the kinds of definitive questions Martha will ask herself, the

kind of inquiries borne of an awareness Albee would like to instill within the spectator. George and Martha will learn that there indeed is no "safety," but in their journey to their own lighthouse, they will learn, as Lily did, to accept their lives without the past negating their present.

The very title of Albee's masterwork is richly symbolic. Invoking the name of one of this century's exemplary novelists invites all sorts of speculation, although Albee tends to downplay the significance of her presence. Albee recalls, in fact, that he first saw what would become the title of his play in a bar (he originally entitled the play *The Exorcism*). "There was a saloon . . . on Tenth Street, between Greenwich Avenue and Waverly Place . . . and they had a big mirror on the downstairs bar in this saloon where people used to scrawl graffiti. At one point back in about 1953 . . . 1954 I think it was—long before any of us started doing much of anything—I was in there having a beer one night, and I saw *Who's Afraid of Virginia Woolf?* scrawled in soap, I suppose, on this mirror. When I started to write the play it cropped up in my mind again" (*CEA,* 52). Perhaps this is why, some eighteen months before the play hit Broadway, Albee quipped, "I'm trying to finish" *Who's Afraid of Virginia Woolf?,* which "is about a two-in-the-morning drunken party of two faculty members and their wives" (*CEA,* 6).

Well beyond the supposed randomness of selecting his play's title, however, looms the wonderful specter of Virginia Woolf. In her diaries, essays, and novels, as in her personal life, Woolf continually explored the gulf, as her friend T. S. Eliot would say, between the idea and the reality, and she naturally gravitated toward the very long shadow between. Like Albee's heroes' tragedies, Virginia Woolf's personal tragedies jarred her sanity. In 1895, after the death of her mother, Woolf experienced the first of several breakdowns. Her father died in 1904, and soon after, Woolf underwent her second breakdown. Within a year after her marriage to Leonard Woolf in 1912 and after *The Voyage Out* was accepted for publication, she again struggled with depression and attempted suicide. By 1915 Virginia Woolf tangled with her most intense mental collapse, and for months appeared raving mad. Her recovery was slow. The years following would see Virginia Woolf ascend to a stature of true brilliance, but the reality of madness hovered ever near the surface of her life and art. By 1940 Virginia Woolf and her husband had drawn plans to commit suicide if Hitler should invade Great Britain, and soon after, their London home was bombed in the Nazi air raids. By 1941, shortly after finishing *Between the Acts,* Virginia Woolf felt the terrifying and all too familiar presence of madness returning. Fearing she might not recover, she composed a loving letter to her husband, filled her pockets with heavy rocks, and drowned herself in the River Ouse.

Albee, in all likelihood, did not compose his masterwork with Virginia Woolf per se on his mind. On the other hand, there is that conspicuous title. To overlook Virginia Woolf's presence in the title and her influence on modern literature in general is to risk missing part of the deeper symbolic resonance emanating from the play. Beyond the nursery rhyme tune of the "Mulberry Bush," whose words are deleted and replaced with the title of the play, remains Virginia Woolf. For Albee's is a play about those reckoning with a lifelong struggle against madness, and one that concerns itself with a Martha who can finally answer the question posed in the play's title by admitting, "I . . . am . . . George. . . . I . . . am. . . ." (242). Like her own fictionalized child, Martha fears life itself. This accounts, too, for Albee's explanation of the play's title. "And of course, who's afraid of Virginia Woolf means who's afraid of the *big bad* wolf . . . who's afraid of living life without false illusions[?]" (*CEA,* 52). The differences between Albee's and Woolf's works, in terms of language, subtlety, and psychology, are vast, and yet certain thematic similarities present themselves in considering Edward Albee and Virginia Woolf.

What is seen and how "the real thing" is knowable, the impending decline of civilization, the combination of lucidity and madness, the fusion of a modernist tradition with new imaginative inventions, death and sexuality—these are just some of the issues to which both writers seem drawn. Albee has said that his task, as artist, centers on dramatizing "imbalance. Most plays are about people out of kilter. . . . I represent what the imbalances are."[3] Woolf elaborated on the same idea years earlier in her well-known "Modern Fiction" essay. "Life is not a series of gig-lamps symmetrically arranged; life is a luminous halo, a semi-transparent envelope surrounding us from the beginning of consciousness to the end."

To the Lighthouse: The Exorcism

And here Woolf anticipated Albee's sense of psychic imbalance. "Is it not the task of the novelist to convey this varying, this unknown and uncircumscribed spirit, whatever aberration or complexity it may display, with as little mixture of the alien and external as possible?"[4]

Perhaps the most compelling link between Virginia Woolf and Edward Albee concerns their preoccupation with *fear*. Woolf's public art mirrored greatly her private reflections, and in *To the Lighthouse*, as elsewhere, she drew upon her own anxieties while sculpting her language and plots. As a child, Virginia Woolf was fearful that the fire in her nursery might flame high enough to touch the wall of her room; in *To the Lighthouse* Cam fears the dancing shadows on the nursery wall; in *Who's Afraid of Virginia Woolf?* the fictional son as a child kept a toy bow and arrow under his bed, we are told, "For fear. Just that: for fear" (219). In her autobiographical work, *Moments of Being*, Woolf reported that her mother, to allay her child's fears at night, would tell Woolf to think of beautiful distractions to get her mind off of the fire; in *To the Lighthouse* Mrs. Ramsey, the mother, does the same thing for Cam, the child. In *Who's Afraid of Virginia Woolf?*, as the exorcism process gains its own momentum, Martha recalls how she comforted her "beautiful, beautiful boy" (220). Fear of the unknown, of psychic dark spaces, of living itself without psychological crutches—these fears paralyze George and Martha, although their ultimate awareness of such ubiquitous fear enables them to rise above its corrosive influence.

> Before they slept, they must fight; after they had fought, they would embrace. From that embrace, another life might be born. But first they must fight, as the dog fights with the vixen, in the heart of darkness, in fields of night.
>
> —Virginia Woolf, *Between the Acts*

Albee's Virginia Woolf–like awareness of and sensitivity to fear informs the exorcism of the play. Whether in praise or scorn, the exorcism that brings the play to a climax has been the source of endless debate. It is also, I believe, the source of the play's theatrical largeness. Throughout the play, as we have now witnessed, Albee has been constantly challenging the audience's sense of logic and what is or is not real. This subversion of audience perception reaches its apogee through the exorcism of the son-myth. But we do not comprehend this until after the fact. Although *after* seeing the play the audience realizes that Albee has worked very carefully to orchestrate what turns out to be the murdering of the son-myth, the audience has no clue (from the performance at least) that the child is anything but real. While seeing the play unwind, live, the audience finds itself caught, like Nick and Honey, in the cross fire, and the furthest thing from our minds is the notion that the child does not live at all. Until Nick's epiphanic moment of comprehension minutes before the play ends—"JESUS CHRIST I THINK I UNDERSTAND THIS!" (236)—we are plainly led to believe that the son lives. No evidence contradicts the notion. The son is mentioned only minutes into the play—"Just don't start in on the bit about the kid," George warns (18)—and will be referred to with growing frequency as each act develops. Even in the midst of exorcising the son-myth, Albee draws upon that very illusion to highlight the mixture of appearances and realities, and to keep the audience's sense of what is verifiable shrouded in mystery. "He is away at school, college," Martha tells us, and "he is fine, everything is fine" (224).

If the audience harbors some doubt about the existence of "the bit," such misgivings seemingly vanish in act 3. For as the play hurtles to its closure, Martha recalls with great clarity her son's birth and early years. There really is nothing too remarkable about a parent recalling the birth of her child; what stands out is the specificity with which Martha retells peak moments of the past. The delivery was difficult but became "an easy birth . . . once it had been . . . accepted, relaxed into" (217). Appearing as if in a trance, Martha goes on to recall other moments, as when he broke his arm and she had to rescue him: "I carried the poor lamb. George snuffling beside me" (221). Other details keep surfacing as Martha, with George, recollects a past filled with happiness.

The meticulous recall of the child confirms his very being-in-the-world. Various portraits of the boy's childhood, from the "antique bassinet from Austria" in his room (218) to the "arrow he kept under his bed" out of "fear" (219), ratify for the audience that, indeed, the boy lives. These details lay to rest any suspicions the audience may have had relative to his place in the world. Even George concedes the point. George, whose levelheadedness maintains the psychic order of the play, announces before all that "the one thing in this whole sinking world that I am sure of is my partnership, my chromosomological partnership in the . . . creation of our . . . blond-eyed, blue-haired . . . son" (72). So all dialogue, all nonverbal gestures, the very intensity and frequency with which George and Martha refer to their child reinforce our conviction that the child lives. This requires no great deduction on the audience's part. Simply put, to think otherwise would be to miss what the characters have been telling us and each other for nearly four hours. *In effect Albee sets us up:* he prepares us for an even greater emotional shock by emphasizing the presence of the illusion that, through the unexpected reversal and subsequent recognition, will explode before our gaze.

In act 3 Albee explores the interstice generated by the truth and illusion matrix. The fictive son assumes a most *real* place within Martha's consciousness during the exorcism. She has a pathological obsession with her child, a fantasy conceived out of her fearful need twenty-one years before to fill a void in her marriage and her own existence. "Oh, I had wanted a child [. . . .] And I had my child," she confides (218). Psychically dependent on her fantasy, she crosses a threshold, for her child does not merely occupy her thoughts—he *possesses* her, like some demon spirit. George knows this and, especially in the final act, sets his sights on one thing: to banish the son-myth interpenetrating his and Martha's world.

George precipitates a ritualized form of expiation through the exorcism performance. Albee mediates the entire third act with a stylized process of expunging what at one time was an innocuous private game but has grown to assume horrific proportions. For Albee wishes the audience to associate the exorcism with the mythological history of past rites of cleansing evil demon spirits inhabiting individuals. Mythologically, an exorcism is a ceremony that attempts to dispel or frighten away evil or demonic forces. Structurally, then, act 3 plays counterpoint to the Walpurgisnacht of act 2. In old German lore, St. Walburga, a British missionary, worked in an eighth-century convent that became one of the chief centers of civilization in Germany. She is often associated with Walpurgisnacht, the May Day festival in which witches reveled in an orgiastic, ritualized Sabbath on Brocken, the tallest peak in the Harz Mountains. Located on the border of East and West Germany, these are rugged, craggy mountains that in St. Walburga's day were thickly forested. During "Walburga's Night" (the witches' Sabbath), as it is called in central Europe, demon spirits are exorcised from villages and villagers by a rite in which a cacophony of loud noises, incense, and holy water are used to achieve purgation. The mysteriousness of all the religious and cultural connotations we bring to our understanding of the exorcism myth and ritual becomes an invisible force, part of the iconography of Albee's play. By invoking the rite of exorcism, Albee broadens the scope of his domestic drama: the sacredness of the unknown, the inscrutability of an existential terror become the mystical screen upon which George and Martha enact their fears. In act 3 demon spirits are first confronted, then externalized through "Bringing Up Baby," and are finally frightened away by the exorcism itself.

In his influential study of myth and ritual, Rene Girard theorizes that sacrifice is essential if community order and harmony are to be restored. "Violence is the heart and secret soul of the sacred," Girard writes in *Violence and the Sacred*.[5] Sacred violence in the form of a ritual sacrifice, suggests Girard, ultimately cleanses the community of violence. Girard develops a fascinating account concerning the relatedness of anthropology, classical tragedy, and Freud; and his ideas about the roles of violence, sacrifice, and the ways in which these forces influence community and spiritual vitality place the violence and exorcism we see in act 3 of *Who's Afraid of Virginia Woolf?* in a positive context. George, by the third act, must come to terms with the sacred violence that he must unleash. Thus, as conductor of the exorcism, George first must discover "some way to really get at" his wife (156), a point that critics often seem to take as proof of the couple's viciousness and hatred for the other. Quite the opposite is the case, I think. To orchestrate the exorcism, George necessarily begins with an invocation to the inner demons released in Walpurgisnacht by enraging Martha to a psychological breaking point. He thereby can bring up the demons for an essentially religious reckoning. Hence the escalation to "Total war" (159). The viciousness of their arguments is a needed ingredient, as Girard might suggest, a method of exteriorizing the unconscious fear, the demons lurking within Martha's psyche.

George arranges fiction to reorder reality. Confiding to Honey news that his "son . . . is . . . DEAD!" (180), George initiates the exorcising process. He discusses the need to "peel labels" (212), a reference to stripping away the emotional attachments blocking Martha from accepting the death of their son. While he seems unsure of his exact procedure, George knows how far the peeling process must go:

> We all peel labels, sweetie; and when you get through the skin, all three layers, through the muscle, slosh aside the organs (*An aside to Nick*) them which is still sloshable—(*Back to Honey*) and get down to bone . . . you know what you do then?
>
> Honey: (*Terribly interested*) No!
>
> George: When you get down to the bone, you haven't got all the way, yet. There's something inside the bone . . . the marrow . . . and that's what you gotta get at. (*A strange smile at Martha*) (212–13)

Symbolically, as George probes from the skin toward the marrow, so, Albee suggests, the aware individual must explore the various levels of consciousness, from the surface to the deeper levels of perception and experience.

Albee creates the image of George-as-surgeon. Like the surgeon, George carefully probes, but into the metaphysical body of his "patient," Martha. As the doctor relies on assistants, so George uses assistants, Nick and Honey, whose unwitting participation in the ritual makes for a successful operation. It is an ontological operation. Throughout, Albee balances the heaviness of the occasion with humorous moments, his method of blending wit and witchcraft, of always decentering the gazing spectator. So it is that a mystified Honey, while in the throes of her own existential awakening and while watching in horror as Martha pours out a lifetime of frustration, can back up George's outrageous story about his son's death-by-car-accident: Yes, she lies, George devoured the Western Union telegram "crazy Billy" delivered, which bore the tragic news (234–35). And the directing force for the metaphysical procedure is *passionate involvement*: to "get at" the marrow means to demystify the child, to excise the illusion, to restore, finally, spiritual health. Although the prognosis for full recovery remains tenuous at best, George takes responsibility for the process.

Playing the game by his rules, George guides Martha through the ritual, providing the objective corrective when needed, the loving assurance when necessary. The dramatic focus is on the depth and power of Martha's psychic attachment to their myth, a child whose existence for twenty-one years counterbalanced the barrenness of their marriage, whose presence was created out of a fear of unfulfillment, an existentialist experience of nothingness.

George evolves from metaphysical surgeon to high priest exorcist. When Martha becomes transfixed on her child and hurts the most, spreading her hands in a crucifixion pose, George recites the Mass of the Dead. Through these hypnotic scenes, Albee places us within "the marrow" of the play. Their illusion shattered by George's latest fiction concerning her son's car accident (the third and final re-presentation of a "Bergin" story), Martha cleanses her soul—"(*A howl which weakens into a moan*): NOOOOOOoooooo" (233)—her purging cry signifying the death of the illusion and the rebirth of some semblance of sanity.

George becomes the celebrant clad in secular vestments. His earlier mention of the "Easter pageant" (208) anticipates the emblematic resurrection that will transpire. He ministers chanted prayers, an offertory series of eucharistic prayers. An incantatory service founded on love, George chants *Kyrie eleison*, invoking the Lord's mercy for the postlapsarian world he and Martha have created. Act 3 becomes a requiem. But this is quite different from Arthur Miller's famous denouement in *Death of a Salesman*. For all the emotionally charged aura surrounding Willy Loman's requiem, Miller distances the audience from the experience. We watch the watchers watching. We *feel* for Willy, of course, but like those attending his funeral, we remain outside *le tourbillion*, the whirlwind, that led Willy to suicide. By contrast, Albee removes the invisible fourth wall within the proscenium arch, enlisting us as active participants in this Mass, a congregation whose very presence actualizes the requiem for the souls of the dead. We become part of the frenzy, rapture, the holy storm.

George recites the Mass of the Dead, its polyphonic quality filling this theater-turned-church. The contrapuntal structure of Martha's English side by side with George's Latin gives the performance a musical quality. "That's a conscious choice of George's to read the Requiem Mass which has existed in Latin for quite a number of years," Albee observes. "I like the sound of the two languages working together. I like the counterpoint of the Latin and the English working together" (*CEA*, 59). This stands as the emotional high point of the entire play, all of the verbal assaults leading to this moment of expiation, a cleansing intensified by George's religious plea for mercy evoked by his *Dies irae* allusion, the portion of the Requiem Mass that describes the judgment and is a prayer to Jesus for divine mercy. Apocalyptic in texture, at once a mixture of a penitential rite and secular plea, the exorcism ushers forth a host of canonical associations.

George's Mass is a performance within a performance. As a parallel to the ritual of the Christian sacrament of the Eucharist, act 3 becomes a secularized enactment of George and Martha's Last Supper with their child and disciples, Nick and Honey. They partake in a communion. The exorcism of the child becomes a reenactment of a crucifixion of the son-myth and paves the way for the resurrection of their own essential selves.

Albee would not wish to push the religious dimension of his play too far. After all, the son is but a fiction created by an all-too-secular couple, and it is not as if generations of religious people have placed their faith in this kid. Still, Albee's script radiates a sense of redemption and secular salvation. There is "*a hint of communion*" in George and Martha's tender exchanges at the play's end (238). Albee himself regards the exorcism as a celebratory occasion: "George and Martha end the play having exorcised some self-created demons and cut away through all nonsense to try to make a relationship based on absolute reality. Strikes me as being a fairly affirmative conclusion to apply" (*CEA*, 152–53).

CODA

> Sometimes a person has to go a very long distance out of his way to
> come back a short distance correctly.
>
> —Jerry in Albee's *The Zoo Story*

The denouement of *Who's Afraid of Virginia Woolf?* suggests that
the son-myth, for now, has vanished. The *"hint of communion"* informing George and Martha's verbal and nonverbal communication implies
the start of a loving armistice, a definitive change in their relationship.
The play's closure, with its Joycean affirmative texture, implies more
than a reconciliation of man and wife; it further implies that they can
now accept their life, its cajoling ambiguity and terrifying flux included,
without illusion. In their resolution, they, and perhaps Nick and Honey,
acknowledge the dread implicit in human existence, and affirm the importance of living honestly. The messy inconclusiveness of the play's closure, then, minimizes sentimentality while functioning thematically:
Albee provides no promise that their marriage will be redeemed, that the
illusion is inexorably shattered. But he does present the very real possibility for a truthful, loving renaissance for his heroes. Their new-tempered
union will be measured in terms of their willingness to keep at bay the illusion that was once a source of happiness but, on this night in New
Carthage, erupted in all its appalling forms.

In *Who's Afraid of Virginia Woolf?*, necessary fictions ultimately
yield to terrifying realities. However, such realities, for Albee the
donnée of human experience, allow George and Martha to accept and,
with acceptance, to love and, with love, to repair the ruins of their past.
Through their long night's journey into day, they have come a very long
distance out of their way to come back a short distance correctly. This
is why the exorcism, indeed the entire play, stands as Albee's valediction
forbidding mourning.

NOTES

1. Historical Context

1. Richard E. Amacher, *Edward Albee*, rev. ed. (Boston: Twayne, 1982), 5.

2. Mas'ud Zavarzadeh, *The Mythopoeic Reality* (Urbana: University of Illinois Press, 1976), 18, 38.

3. Alice van Buren Kelley, *"To the Lighthouse": The Marriage of Life and Art* (Boston: Twayne, 1987), 2.

4. Introduction, *Edward Albee: A Collection of Critical Essays*, ed. C. W. E. Bigsby (Englewood Cliffs, N.J.: Prentice-Hall, 1975), 4.

5. Bigsby, Introduction, 5.

6. Matthew C. Roudané, "An Interview with Arthur Miller," *Conversations with Arthur Miller*, ed. Matthew C. Roudané (Jackson and London: University Press of Mississippi, 1987), 374.

7. Matthew C. Roudané, "An Interview with David Mamet," *Studies in American Drama, 1945–Present* 1 (1986):79.

8. Daniel Blum, *Theatre World: Season 1962–1963*, vol. 19 (New York: Chilton Books, 1963), 6.

9. Jack Poggi, *Theater in America: The Impact of Economic Forces, 1870–1967*, (Ithaca, N.Y.: Cornell University Press, 1968), 46–49.

10. Walter J. Meserve, *Heralds of Promise: The Drama of the American People during the Age of Jackson, 1829–1849* (Westport, Conn.: Greenwood Press, 1986), 8.

11. Frank Rich, "To Make Serious Theater 'Serious' Issues Aren't Enough," *New York Times*, 19 February 1984, quoted in Thomas P. Adler, *Mirror on the Stage* (West Lafayette: Purdue University Press, 1987), ix.

12. Martin Esslin, " 'Dead! And Never Called Me Mother!': The Missing Dimension in American Drama," in Matthew C. Roudané, ed., *Studies in the Literary Imagination* 21 (1988): 31. For additional excellent discussions of this point, see Herbert Blau, "Hysteria, Crabs, Gospel, and Random Access: Ring Around the Audience," in *Studies in the Literary Imagination*, 7–21; and Adler, *Mirror of the Stage*, ix–xiv.

2. The Importance of the Work

1. Roudané, "An Interview with Arthur Miller," 374.

2. Blau, "Hysteria, Crabs, Gospel, and Random Access: Ring Around the Audience," 16.

3. C. W. E. Bigsby, *A Critical Introduction to Twentieth-Century American Drama* (New York: Cambridge University Press, 1984), 2:1.

4. John Barth, quoted in Charles B. Harris, *Passionate Virtuosity: The Fiction of John Barth* (Urbana: University of Illinois Press, 1983), x.

5. Alan Prince, "An Interview with John Barth," *Prism* (1968):62.

3. Critical Reception

1. Bigsby, *A Critical Introduction*, 2:265.

2. Edward Albee, "Wants to Know Why," *New York Times*, 7 October 1962, 1, 3.

3. Gilbert Debusscher, *Edward Albee: Tradition and Renewal*, trans. Anne D. Williams (Brussels: Center for American Studies, 1967), 47.

4. Howard Taubman, "Cure for Blues," *New York Times*, 28 October 1962, 1.

5. Robert Coleman, "The Play You'll Love to Loathe," *New York Daily Mirror*, 15 October 1962, 20.

6. Robert Brustein, "Albee and the Medusa-Head," *New Republic*, 3 November 1962, 29–30.

7. Harold Clurman, *"Who's Afraid of Virginia Woolf?,"* in *A Collection of Critical Essays*, 77, 78.

8. Dianna Trilling, "The Riddle of Albee's *Who's Afraid of Virginia Woolf?,"* in *A Collection of Critical Essays*, 85.

9. Richard Schechner, "Who's Afraid of Edward Albee?," in *A Collection of Critical Essays*, 63.

10. W. H. von Dreele, "The 20th Century and All That . . . ," *National Review*, 15 January 1963, 35–36.

11. Richard A. Duprey, *"Who's Afraid of Virginia Woolf?,"* *Catholic World* (January 1963):263, 264.

12. John McCarten, "Long Night's Journey into Daze," *New Yorker*, 20 October 1962, 85.

13. J. C. Trewin, "Nights with the Ripsaw," *The Illustrated London News*, 22 February 1964, 288.

14. Richard Watts, "Two on the Aisle: Shattering Play by Edward Albee," *New York Post*, 25 January 1961, 14.

Notes

15. John Gassner, "Broadway in Review," *Educational Theatre Journal* 15 (March 1963):80.

16. Mel Gussow, "Game of Truth," *Newsweek*, 29 October 1962, 52.

17. For further details, see Wendell V. Harris, "Morality, Absurdity, and Albee," *Southwest Review* 29 (1964):249–256.

18. Jonas Barish, "Shakespeare in the Study; Shakespeare on the Stage," *Theatre Journal* 40 (March 1988):46.

19. Anne Paolucci, *From Tension to Tonic: The Plays of Edward Albee* (Carbondale: Southern Illinois University Press, 1972), 15.

20. Ruby Cohn, *Currents in Contemporary Drama* (Bloomington: Indiana University Press, 1969), 72.

21. Bigsby, *A Critical Introduction*, 2:327.

22. Thomas P. Adler, "Art or Craft: Language in the Plays of Albee's Second Decade," in *Edward Albee: Planned Wilderness*, ed. Patricia De La Fuente, Living Authors Series No. 3 (Edinburg, Texas: Pan American University Press, 1980), 45.

23. George Wellwarth, *The Theatre of Protest and Paradox* (New York: New York University Press, 1964), 284.

24. Ihab Hassan, *Contemporary American Literature* (New York: Ungar, 1973), 152.

25. Paolucci, *From Tension to Tonic*, 46.

26. Debusscher, *Tradition and Renewal*, 57, 82, 83.

27. C. W. E. Bigsby, *Edward Albee* (Edinburgh: Oliver and Boyd, 1969), 9, 21, 96.

28. Ruby Cohn, *Edward Albee* (Minneapolis: University of Minnesota Press, 1969), 6.

29. Paolucci, *From Tension to Tonic*, 3.

30. Anita Marie Stenz, *Edward Albee: The Poet of Loss* (The Hague: Mouton, 1978), 132.

31. Bigsby, *A Critical Introduction*, 2:328, 264.

32. For a detailed bibliographic survey of Albee scholarship, see Anne Paolucci, "Edward Albee," *American Dramatists*, ed. Matthew C. Roudané (Detroit: Gale Research Co., 1989), 3–47.

4. Toward the Marrow

1. "Blood Sport," *Time*, 26 October 1962, 84.

2. Harold Bloom, Introduction, *Edward Albee: Modern Critical Views* (New Haven: Chelsea House, 1987), 6, 8.

3. Bigsby, *A Critical Introduction*, 2:271.

4. Matthew C. Roudané, "An Interview with Edward Albee," *Southern Humanities Review* 16 (1982):38.

6. Madness

1. Roudané, "An Interview with Edward Albee," 38.

2. Blau, "Hysteria, Crabs, Gospel, and Random Access: Ring Around the Audience," 10.

3. Matthew C. Roudané, "Albee on Albee," *RE: Artes Liberales* 10 (1984):1–2.

4. June Schlueter, *Metafictional Characters in Modern Drama* (New York: Columbia University Press, 1979), 86.

7. Toward the Marrow

1. Roudané, "An Interview with Edward Albee," 41, 43.

2. Antonin Artaud, *The Theatre and Its Double*, trans. Mary C. Richards (New York: Grove Press, 1958), 41.

3. Matthew C. Roudané, "A Playwright Speaks: An Interview with Edward Albee," *Critical Essays on Edward Albee*, ed. Philip C. Kolin and J. Madison Davis (Boston: G. K. Hall, 1986), 195.

4. Ibid., 194.

5. Cohn, *Currents in Contemporary Drama*, 72.

6. Bigsby, *A Critical Introduction*, 2:327.

7. Julian Beck, "Storming the Barricades," in Kenneth H. Brown, *The Brig* (New York: Hill and Wang, 1965), 7, 9, 18.

8. Roudané, "A Playwright Speaks," 198.

8. The Characters

1. Bigsby, *A Critical Introduction*, 2:250.

2. Virginia Woolf, *Moments of Being: Unpublished Autobiographical Writings*, ed. Jeanne Shulkind (New York and London: Harcourt Brace Jovanovich, rev. ed., 1985), 116.

3. William Barrett, *What Is Existentialism?* (New York: Grove Press, 1964), 58–59.

4. Ibid., 59.

5. Uta Hagen, *Respect for Acting* (New York: Macmillan, 1973), 170.

6. Barrett, *What Is Existentialism?*, 59.

Notes

7. Hagen, *Respect for Acting*, 163–64.

8. Stenz, *The Poet of Loss*, 43.

9. Emil Roy, "*Who's Afraid of Virginia Woolf?* and the Tradition," in *Critical Essays on Edward Albee*, 93.

10. Roudané, "An Interview with Edward Albee," 39.

11. Paolucci, *From Tension to Tonic*, 52.

12. Ibid., 61.

13. Arthur Schlesinger, "Tocqueville and American Democracy," *Michigan Quarterly Review* 25 (1986):495.

14. Michael E. Rutenberg, *Edward Albee: Playwright in Protest* (New York: Avon, 1969), 212.

15. Schlesinger, "Tocqueville and American Democracy," 499.

16. Ibid., 495.

17. Laura Julier, "Faces to the Dawn: Female Characters in Albee's Plays," in *Edward Albee: Planned Wilderness*, 37.

18. Bigsby, *A Critical Introduction*, 2:250.

9. The Set and Setting

1. Martin Esslin, *An Anatomy of Drama* (New York: Hill and Wang, 1976), 65.

2. Bigsby, *A Critical Introduction*, 2:264.

3. Paolucci, *From Tension to Tonic*, 45.

4. Bigsby, *A Critical Introduction*, 2:277–78.

5. Ibid., 273.

6. Amacher, *Edward Albee*, 72.

7. Esslin, *An Anatomy of Drama*, 53.

10. The Exorcism

1. van Buren Kelley, "*To the Lighthouse*": *The Marriage of Life and Art*, 6.

2. Virginia Woolf, *To the Lighthouse* (New York and London: Harcourt Brace Jovanovich, rpr., 1955), 268.

3. Roudané, "An Interview with Edward Albee," 38.

4. Virginia Woolf, *Collected Essays*, vol. 2, ed. Leonard Woolf (New York: Harcourt, Brace & World, 1967), 106.

5. Rene Girard, *Violence and the Sacred*, trans. Patrick Gregory (Baltimore: Johns Hopkins University Press, 1977), 31.

SELECTED BIBLIOGRAPHY

Primary Works

Plays

"Schism." *The Choate Literary Magazine* 20 (1946):87–110.

The Zoo Story and The American Dream. New York: Signet, 1960.

The Zoo Story, The Death of Bessie Smith, The Sandbox. New York: Coward-McCann, 1960.

The American Dream. New York: Coward-McCann, 1961.

Who's Afraid of Virginia Woolf? New York: Atheneum, 1962; London: Jonathan Cape, 1964.

The Sandbox, The Death of Bessie Smith, with Fam and Yam. New York: New American Library, 1963.

Tiny Alice. New York: Atheneum, 1965; London: Jonathan Cape, 1966.

A Delicate Balance. New York: Atheneum, 1966; London: Jonathan Cape, 1968.

Box and Quotations from Chairman Mao Tse-tung. New York: Atheneum, 1969; London: Jonathan Cape, 1970.

All Over. New York: Atheneum, 1971; London: Jonathan Cape, 1972.

Seascape. New York: Atheneum, 1975; London: Jonathan Cape, 1976.

Counting the Ways and Listening. New York: Atheneum, 1977.

The Lady from Dubuque. New York: Atheneum, 1980.

The Plays, vol. 1. New York: Coward, McCann, and Geoghegan, 1981.

The Plays, vol. 2. New York: Atheneum, 1983.

The Plays, vol. 3. New York: Atheneum, 1983.

The Plays, vol. 4. New York: Atheneum, 1983.

"Finding the Sun." Unpublished, 1983.

"Walking." Unpublished, 1984.

The Man Who Had Three Arms. New York: Atheneum, 1987.

"Marriage Play." Unpublished, 1987.

Selected Bibliography

Adaptations

"Bartleby." Unpublished libretto adaption of Herman Melville's short story.

Malcolm. New York: Atheneum, 1966; London: Jonathan Cape, 1967. Adaptation of James Purdy's novel.

The Ballad of the Sad Café. Boston: Houghton Miffin, 1963; London: Jonathan Cape, 1965. Adaptation of Carson McCullers's novella.

Breakfast at Tiffany's. Music by Bob Merrill. Produced in Philadelphia, 1966. Musical adaptation of Truman Capote's novel.

Everything in the Garden. New York: Atheneum, 1968. Adaptation of Giles Cooper's play.

Lolita. New York: Dramatist Play Service, 1984. Adaptation of the Vladimir Nabokov novel.

Envy. Vignette. Part of Nagel Jackson's *Faustus in Hell*. January 1985.

Unpublished/Unperformed Plays

The manuscripts of these plays are held at the New York Public Library at Lincoln Center and may be seen only after Albee himself grants special permission. They are not intended for performance. (This information is from C. W. E. Bigsby, *Edward Albee: Bibliography, Biography, Playography*, Theatre Checklist No. 22 (London: TQ Publications, 1980), 4–6.)

"The City of People" (1949). 177-page manuscript.

"Untitled Play" (perhaps *In A Quiet Room*, 1949). Thirty-four-page manuscript.

"Ye Watchers and Ye Lonely Ones" (1951).

"The Invalid" (1952). Eighteen-page manuscript.

"The Making of a Saint" (1953–54). Seventy-six-page manuscript.

"The Ice Age" (undated). Thirty-five-page manuscript.

"An End to Summer" (undated). Forty-page manuscript.

Untitled Play (perhaps *The Recruit*, undated). Nine-page manuscript.

"Untitled Opera" (perhaps *Hatchet, Hatchet*, undated).

Short Stories

"L'Apres-midi d'un faune." *Choate Literary Magazine* 31 (1945):43–44.

"Empty Tea." *Choate Literary Magazine* 31 (1945):53–59.

"A Place on the Water." *Choate Literary Magazine* 32(1945):15–18.

"Well, It's Like This." *Choate Literary Magazine* 32 (1945):31–34.

"Lady with an Umbrella." *Choate Literary Magazine* 32 (1946):5–10.

"A Novel Beginning." *Esquire* 60 (1963):59–60.

Poetry

"Old Laughter." *Choate Literary Magazine* 31 (1944):37–38.

"To a Gold Chain Philosopher at Luncheon." *Choate Literary Magazine* 31 (1945):34.

"To Whom It May Concern." *Choate Literary Magazine* 31 (1945):61.

"Associations." *Choate Literary Magazine* 31 (1945):15–16.

"Frustration." *Choate Literary Magazine* 31 (1945):60.

"Questions." *Choate Literary Magazine* 31 (1945):81.

"Monologue," "The Atheist," and "Sonnet," *Choate Literary Magazine* 32 (1945):10.

"Reunion." *Choate Literary Magazine* 32 (1945):71–72.

"Eighteen." *Kaleidograph* 17 (1945):15.

"Interlude." *Choate Literary Magazine* 32 (1946):29.

"To a Maniac," *Choate Literary Magazine* 32 (1946):71.

"Nihilist." *Choate Literary Magazine* 32 (1946):22.

"Peaceable Kingdom, France." *The New Yorker,* 29 December 1975, 34.

Nonfiction

"Richard Strauss." *Choate Literary Magazine* 31 (1945):87–93.

"Chaucer: The Legend of Phyllis." *Choate Literary Magazine* 32 (1945): 59–63.

"What's It About?—a Playwright Tries to Tell." *New York Herald Tribune Magazine,* "The Lively Arts," 22 January 1961, 5.

"Which Theatre Is the Absurd One?" *New York Times Magazine,* 25 February 1962, 30–31, 64, 66.

"Some Notes on Non-Conformity." *Harper's Bazaar,* August 1962, 104.

"Carson McCullers—the Case of the Curious Magician." *Harper's Bazaar,* January 1963, 98.

Review of Lillian Ross's novel *Vertical and Horizontal. Village Voice,* 11 July 1963, 1.

"Who's Afraid of the Truth?" *New York Times,* arts section, 18 August 1963, 1.

"Ad Libs on Theater." *Playbill,* May 1965.

Review of Sam Shepard's *Icarus's Mother. Village Voice,* 25 November 1965, 19.

Introduction to *Three Plays by Noel Coward.* New York: Dell, 1965.

"Who Is James Purdy?" *New York Times,* arts section, 9 January 1966, 1, 3.

"Creativity and Commitment." *Saturday Review,* 4 June 1966, 26.

"Judy Garland." In *Double Exposure,* ed. Roddy McDowell, 198–99. New York: Delacorte, 1966.

"Apartheid in the Theater." *New York Times,* arts section, 30 July 1967, 1, 6.

Selected Bibliography

"Albee Says 'No Thanks' to John Simon." *New York Times*, arts section, 10 September 1967, 1, 8.

"The Decade of Engagement." *Saturday Review*, 24 January 1970, 19–20.

"The Future Belongs to Youth." *New York Times*, arts section, 26 November 1971, 1.

"Albeit." In *The Off-Broadway Experience*, ed. Howard Greenberger, 52–62. Englewood Cliffs, N.J.: Prentice-Hall, 1971.

"Edward Albee on Louise Nevelson: The World Is Beginning to Resemble Her Art." *Art News* (1980):99–101.

Foreword to *Dream Palaces* by James Purdy. New York: Viking, 1980, vii–ix.

Secondary Works

Bibliographies

Amacher, Richard E., and Margaret Rule. *Edward Albee at Home and Abroad*. New York: AMS Press, 1973. Primary and secondary.

Bigsby, C. W. E. *Edward Albee: Bibliography, Biography, Playography*. Theatre Checklist No. 22. London: TQ Publications, 1980. Primary and secondary.

Giantvalley, Scott. *Edward Albee: A Reference Guide*. Boston: G. K. Hall, 1987. Primary and secondary; contains nearly 2,700 entries.

Green, Charles. *Edward Albee: An Annotated Bibliography, 1968–1977*. New York: AMS Press, 1980. Primary and secondary.

King, Kimball. *Ten Modern American Playwrights: An Annotated Bibliography*, 1–108. New York: Garland, 1982. Primary and secondary.

Tyce, Richard. *Edward Albee: A Bibliography*. Metuchen, N.J.: Scarecrow Press, 1986. Primary and secondary.

Books, Chapters of Books, and Essays

Adler, Thomas P. "Albee's *Virginia Woolf*: A Long Night's Journey into Day." *Educational Theatre Journal* 25 (1973):66–70. Sees George's exorcism of the child as the replacing of one reality with another; Martha will depend on George's strength as a defense against her fear of the unknown.

Amacher, Richard E. *Edward Albee*. Rev. ed. Boston: Twayne, 1982. Careful explication of each play through *Lolita;* contains biographical background material and a discussion of Albee's dramatic theories.

Bigsby, C. W. E. *Albee*. Edinburgh: Oliver and Boyd, 1969. Identifies Albee's liberal humanistic concerns; by one of the world's leading Albee scholars.

————, ed. *Edward Albee*. Englewood Cliffs, N.J.: Prentice-Hall, 1975. Provocative introduction and twenty-one essays, reviews, and interviews.

————. *A Critical Introduction to Twentieth-Century American Drama*. Vol. 2. Cambridge: Cambridge University Press, 1984. One-third of book devoted to Albee. Considers in detail Albee's early, unpublished material. Excellent.

Bloom, Harold, ed. *Edward Albee: Modern Critical Views*. New Haven, Conn.: Chelsea House, 1987. Contains eleven essays and Bloom's introduction.

Braem, Helmut M. *Edward Albee*. Hannover, Germany: Velber Verlag, 1968. Useful European perspective; in German.

Cohn, Ruby. *Edward Albee*. Minneapolis: University of Minnesota Press, 1969. Excellent.

————. *Currents in Contemporary Drama*. Bloomington: Indiana University Press, 1969. Focuses on Albee's accusative dialogues.

Debusscher, Gilbert. *Edward Albee: Tradition and Renewal*, translated by Anne D. Williams. Brussels: American Studies Center, 1967. Discusses the European influence on Albee's aesthetic; concludes that Albee is a nihilist.

De La Fuente, Patricia, ed. *Edward Albee: Planned Wilderness: Interviews, Essays, and Bibliography*. Living Author Series No. 3. Edinburg, Texas: Pan American University, 1980. Eight essays, an interview, and a bibliography.

Hayman, Ronald. *Edward Albee*. New York: Ungar, 1971. Explicates each play.

Hirsch, Foster. *Who's Afraid of Edward Albee?* Berkeley, Calif. Creative Arts Book, 1978. Interprets the plays from a biographical viewpoint; discusses the influence of Albee's homosexuality on the characters.

Kerjan, Lillian. *Albee*. Paris: Seghers, 1971. In French.

————. *Le Théâtre d'Edward Albee*. Paris: Klincksieck, 1979. In French.

Kolin, Philip, and J. Madison Davis, eds. *Critical Essays on Edward Albee*. Boston: G. K. Hall, 1986. Includes thirty-nine essays, interviews, reviews. Features comprehensive bibliographic essay on Albee scholarship.

Kolin, Philip C., ed. *Conversations with Edward Albee*. Jackson and London: University Press of Mississippi, 1988. Contains twenty-seven interviews.

McCarthy, Gerry. *Edward Albee*. New York: St. Martin's, 1987. Considers selected plays from performance perspective.

Otten, Terry. *After Innocence: Visions of the Fall in Modern Literature*, 174–91. Pittsburgh: Pittsburgh University Press, 1982. Discussion of *Virginia Woolf*.

Paolucci, Anne. *From Tension to Tonic: The Plays of Edward Albee*. Carbondale: Southern Illinois University Press, 1972. Posits that language is Albee's major contribution; one of the best studies on Albee; considers the existentialist dimension of the plays.

Selected Bibliography

———. "Albee and the Restructuring of the Modern Stage." *Studies in American Drama* 1 (Summer 1986):4–16. Explains Albee's experiments with dramatic language and structure.

Roudané, Matthew C. *Understanding Edward Albee*. Columbia: University of South Carolina Press, 1987. Discusses nine plays while tracing Albee's affirmative existentialist vision.

———, ed. *American Dramatists*, 3–47. Detroit: Gale Research Co., 1989. Paolucci's bibliographic essay on Albee.

Rutenberg, Michael E. *Edward Albee: Playwright in Protest*. New York: Avon, 1969. Sees Albee as highly political writer whose plays are, above all, social protest works; includes two interviews.

Schlueter, June. *Metafictional Characters in Modern Drama*, 79–87. New York: Columbia University Press, 1979. Excellent focus on the fictive and real identities of George and Martha in *Virginia Woolf*.

Schultz-Seitz, Ruth Eva. *Edward Albee, der Dichterphilosoph der Buhne*. Frankfurt-am-Main: Vittorio Klostermann, 1966. In German.

Stenz, Anita Marie. *Edward Albee: The Poet of Loss*. The Hague: Mouton, 1978. Argues that Albee challenges the buffers or illusions people create to shield themselves from reality; a solid study that concentrates on the characters' psychologies.

Wasserman, Julian N., ed. *Edward Albee: An Interview and Essays*. Lee Lecture Series, University of St. Thomas, Houston. Syracuse, N.Y.: Syracuse University Press, 1983. Includes lengthy interview with Albee and eight essays.

INDEX

Index

Index

ABOUT THE AUTHOR

Matthew C. Roudané is associate professor of English at Georgia State University in Atlanta, where he teaches modern drama and American literature. His books include *Understanding Edward Albee* (1987), *Conversations with Arthur Miller* (1987), and *American Dramatists* (1989), and he has edited *Studies in the Literary Imagination,* a collection of critical essays on contemporary American theater and drama (1988). He is also editor of *Approaches to Teaching Miller's 'Death of a Salesman,'* which is part of the Modern Language Association's Approaches to Teaching World Masterpieces Series (forthcoming). His numerous essays, interviews, book and theater reviews have appeared in such journals as *American Literature, Modern Drama, Modern Philology,* and the *Michigan Quarterly Review.* Roudané, who serves on the editorial or advisory boards of six scholarly journals, has taught at the University of Oregon and Emory University.